Handbook to Happiness

TYNDALE HOUSE
Publishers, Inc.
Wheaton, Illinois

Handbook to Happiness

by Charles R. Solomon, Ed.D

A Guide to Victorious Living and Effective Counseling

Author's note: The Scripture references quoted are from the King James Version unless otherwise noted.

Library of Congress Card No. 75-29863
ISBN 8423-1280-3
Third printing, Tyndale House edition April, 1977

DEDICATION
*To my wife, Sue, who has
shared and suffered with me as
my life was shaped on God's
anvil that I might begin to be
"conformed to his image."*

CONTENTS

FOREWORD

The purpose of this foreword is twofold: to introduce and endorse the concepts herein presented, and to provide endorsement from a different discipline.

When Dr. Solomon came to Grand Rapids in November 1974 a new horizon opened for that city. He presented the truth of the victory and triumph a believer can be brought into through understanding the cross as a place not only where Christ died but where the *old self* was crucified, buried, and raised in newness of life, thence seated with him.

Having begun my own career in medicine as a family physician in Wisconsin, I was soon led to see that human needs were more than physical. The emotional needs of my patients were encountered daily. Formal psychiatric residency gave me new credentials and qualifications to meet these needs.

Following this training, I received an offer to serve as Medical Director at the Mental Health Center in Grand Rapids, Michigan. Many times I have had the opportunity to help people but also many times I ran into dead ends as "insight" provided understanding but left people essentially powerless to utilize that new information—to harness it to a reliable power source so they could move ahead. Many "new" methods of treatment were devised, only to find recurrence and chronicity a haunting plague. Was there not a better way? Was there not something more?

Within myself, during this time, there was a spirit of unrest. I knew I was saved. I served the Lord, preaching when the opportunity arose, and serving on various boards. I was active in evangelical outreach but down deep there remained a yearning, a spiritual thirst for a deeper life, an "abundant life," a life of victory and triumph rather than the ups and downs of living and doing the best I could for the Lord. I found surrender not enough. Turning over new leaves, and trying harder with new resolutions only left recurrent defeat. There had to be a way—there is—but it lies *outside myself*.

Then came the truth of the *cross*, the "exchanged life," the co-crucifixion with Christ as the liberating *key* that unlocked the secret of struggle. I have seen it work in lives where traditional methods have failed. This *key* is presented well by Dr. Solomon and provides liberation and freedom as the Spirit of God brings victory.

I wholeheartedly recommend Dr. Solomon's treatise as the *key* not only to personal victory but the answer to those who are seeking to help others.

PAUL E. KASCHEL, M.D.

PREFACE

This book is written by a layman for laymen or for anyone else who is looking for an answer—not an argument. It is intentionally informal in style and is written in language the person unschooled in theological jargon can understand. It is a practical handbook, not a profound theological treatise, and should be read as such. It is necessarily brief and merely gives the core of this approach; subsequent writing will explore it in greater detail.

Sincere inquiries regarding the appropriation of the victorious life are invited and will be answered as time permits.

CHARLES R. SOLOMON

ACKNOWLEDGMENTS

I owe a debt of gratitude to my pastor Rev. Burton C. Murdock, not only for his loyal support, prayer, and advice but also for reading the manuscript and making valuable suggestions.

My appreciation also goes to my dear friends, Dr. Robert Walden and Dr. Raymond Buker for their help in reading the entire manuscript and contributing to it. Leslie Walden, Jo Wade, Florence Stevens, and my sister, Camilla Hurst, rendered valuable assistance in typing and re-typing the manuscript.

And, last but not least, to my family for their patience during the writing, I say a humble "Thank you."

PROLOGUE

Spirituotherapy® is a new discipline which is
being pioneered by Grace Fellowship
International (GFI). This organization was
incorporated in the state of Colorado in 1969 as a
non-profit corporation for the express purpose of
implementing a spiritual counseling ministry. As
such, it has been accepted as a member of the
National Association of Evangelicals and
recognized as a tax-exempt religious organization
by the Internal Revenue Service. It is
interdenominational in scope, and its
allegiance is to the Lord Jesus Christ and to the
infallible and immutable Word of God.

Dr. Solomon, who is the founder and
executive director of GFI, received his B.S.
degree from East Tennessee State University
and the Master of Personnel Service degree from
the University of Colorado. He earned the
Doctor of Education degree from the
University of Northern Colorado. Much of the
work toward this degree was in original research,
counseling, writing, and teaching associated
with the discipline of Spirituotherapy; the
remainder was in counseling and psychology.

Dr. Solomon began counseling part time while
employed in the aerospace industry by Martin
Marietta Corporation, his sole employer since
completing undergraduate work in 1951. He also
did some counseling in the industrial setting
under an MA-3 contract with the Department of
Labor where Martin Marietta was to hire and
train "hard-core unemployed" females for

[15]

clerical work. His master's thesis was based on the results of that program. The thesis is entitled "Use of the Critical Incident Technique to Study Changes in Behavior During an Industrial Training Program for Disadvantaged Persons Where Counseling with Optional Spiritual Guidance Was an Integral Part of the Program." Although the philosophy of counseling and the spiritual qualifications of the counselor were not given in any detail, the results are well documented and speak for themselves.

The first GFI office opened on 1 February 1970. There has been no subsidization from the beginning to the present, and the clientele has increased to the point where additional counselors have been added to the staff. As of 1977 the thrust of the ministry is that of counselor training with each individual responsible to the Lord for his place of ministry. Centers for training other than Denver may be opened as God leads.

HEART TO HEART

When we come to the place of full retreat
    And our heart cries out for God,
The only person whose heart ours can meet
    Is the one who has likewise trod.

Others may offer a word of cheer
    To lift us from despair;
But above the rest, the one we hear
    Is the whisper, "I've been there."

                                    C. R. SOLOMON

NEW HELP FOR OLD PROBLEMS

As we are confronted with human misery we sometimes cry out, "How can we help those who are lonely and searching to find purpose and peace in this life?" In the counseling setting as we have opportunity to share with those in need, we find persons of all ages, educational levels, and cultural backgrounds presenting the same basic problem—the lack of a deeply satisfying existence.

Persons representing every discipline (and no discipline) are forwarding theories about human behavior in a futile attempt to bring order out of chaos. Various behavioristic approaches proffered by both the secular and religious communities aim to lead individuals and groups to tranquility and fulfillment. Most of these approaches require great outlays of capital and depend solely on human resources for their implementation. Since most of these are based on the temporal, rather than the eternal, the results will be ephemeral, if not a total waste of time. The dissatisfaction of young and old alike, which contributes to the unsettled condition in this country and the world, is attributed to such things as lack of education, lack of opportunity, oppression of minorities, unemployment, prejudice, bigotry, and other popular catchalls. These are all merely symptoms of a deeper problem which most persons are unwilling to face objectively. It is so much easier to cop out and blame others, society, another race, the young generation or the Establishment than it is to see

[17]

things as they are. It is much more popular to start great programs for symptomatic treatment than to get to the root of the problem. The vast expenditures of private and federal funds on "mental health" is the epitome of such an exercise in futility. As will be pointed out subsequently, mental difficulties are symptoms—not problems. It is somewhat comforting to have the symptoms eased, but it does nothing to meet the underlying problem. It is necessary, therefore, to redouble the effort and quadruple the expenditure of funds in a vain effort to keep the symptoms under control.

Some weary of working with the details in individual lives and attempt to generalize and group the symptoms. Two such groupings are the *generation gap* and the *identity crisis*. First, let us look at the rationale behind the generation gap and its role in explaining the societal problems which are extant.

Generation Gap

Much is made of the so-called "generation gap" and the ludicrous supposition that a person over thirty has no hope of communicating with the younger generation. This is one of the biggest frauds that has ever been perpetrated. Contrary to popular belief, the passing of years, whether it be few or many, has no effect whatever on the basic needs of the human heart. There is no difference in this regard within generations or between them, whether they be separated by years or centuries.

When faced from a purely humanistic and materialistic viewpoint, there *is* a disparity in goals that is difficult if not impossible to bridge. This is the inevitable price we pay for forsaking our spiritual heritage which is the great common denominator. The younger generation is inclined to reject any set of values which affirms that happiness and fulfillment are the result of wealth and material things. A hedonistic philosophy based on materialism turns them off. Most younger people, however, do not realize that their value system is also based on materialism—a negation of the materialistic with nothing positive to replace it. In fact, it is hypocritical since it is a subculture which depends on the society it condemns for its very existence.

Neither the materialistic Establishment system nor the anti-materialistic youth subculture has, of itself, what is most vital to meet the deepest needs of man. Each has its own ways of escaping from the inevitable emptiness of a system that tacitly or blatantly denies God his proper place, individually and collectively.

The older generation may use alcohol and tranquilizers when the pursuit of pleasure ceases to dull the mind to the futility of such an existence. It takes the younger generation considerably less time to find that there is little real fulfillment after the kicks of rebellion have worn off. That is why many resort to drugs and become slaves to them rather than to the Establishment. Becoming addicted, they pursue every illegal or questionable means to obtain funds from the Establishment to support their habits. Thus, the cycle is completed where the subculture is again dependent upon the very system which it holds in contempt.

It should come as no surprise that a materialistic culture which leaves its subjects empty should spawn another culture which is equally incapable of meeting the deepest needs of its adherents. Of the two, the original

[19]

culture bears the greater condemnation. And yet, self-righteous Establishment persons, who may be using alcohol or tranquilizers to inhibit the effects of an illicit sexual relationship, will berate a young person on drugs who is engaging in "free love." It is little wonder that each thinks the other is a hypocrite!

More and more, young people are beginning to turn on to various ideologies, religions, the mystical, to the cults and to the occult in an attempt to find meaning beyond this life and to fill the inner spiritual vacuum. Some are finding reality and some are merely finding a mindbender without the use of drugs. The over-thirty group is beginning to wake up to the fact that adverse ideologies and a shaky ecology are about to render useless the myriad of things which make up the hedonistic or "good life."

At GFI we find no bridgeless "generation gap" since the same answer applies to all, regardless of age or the particular situation which becomes unbearable and forces the person to come for counseling.

Another phrase which describes a portion of the emptiness syndrome is the "identity crisis."

Identity Crisis

Another mistaken notion that has been palmed off on the public is that the younger generation is unique in its identity crisis. In one sense this is true. Generally speaking, the young people do not know who they are. Many are very outspoken in admitting it. Those who are "doing their own thing" in the most bizarre fashions are actively, if not knowingly, searching for an identity which gives meaning to life. In this pursuit they are only different from their parents in one main particular—they admit it and their parents do not. Most youth are honest enough to question the heritage (?) their parents have left, even though their query often gains them more trouble than the initial situation.

It is equally true that the parents also are in an identity crisis. The prime difference is that the older generation does not know it or will not admit it. They do not have *firsthand* knowledge of who they are, so they are still living out a role their parents assigned them. The role is somewhat comfortable in that it is well supplied with material things; and the behavior is socially acceptable, if not spiritually. At least there is the attempt to be discreet and not advertise the cheating on income tax, alcoholism, wife-swapping, destroying another person in business, kick-backs on sales, narcissism in politics, and other behavior patterns which are not as visible as the "do your own thing" approach of the young people. These same parents are horrified when their children reject their "good" middle-class values in favor of a life of near-poverty, drugs, long hair, and open sex. They will try everything (except prayer) and lament, "I've done so much for them and given them everything. How can they possibly do this to *me*?" Many times the parents are more concerned about the effect on their own image than that their child's life is being destroyed. The older generation is still living on a borrowed set of values which have at best "a form of godliness but denying the power thereof" (2 Timothy 3:5). This identity was not sufficient for them or there would not be the wholesale use of alcohol and tranquilizers and pursuit of pleasure.

The identity crisis really started back two generations where those in their forties today did not receive from their parents an active faith in Jesus Christ. Consequently, they are living on "second hand" Christianity, if it can be called Christianity at all. At least there is enough moral fiber to produce socially acceptable behavior in the main. The spiritual vacuum, however, which they have passed along to their children has become a way of life, and they cannot understand why their children overtly reject it. They will not be honest enough to admit openly that it doesn't even satisfy themselves!

So we have two generations in an identity crisis, one that knows it and one that doesn't, condemning each other for their misguided attempts to find a purposeful existence. Both generations have founded their identities on materialism, positive and negative, but the younger generation is running into a problem that is more acute than that of their parents—the accelerated pace with which everything is changing. The older generation identifies with the middle class suburban culture, and, until recently, this has remained fairly stable. In other words, their identity was, and is, based on peer group values. As long as these are fairly constant, at least the identity is clear in that context. The young people, however, are not nearly so fortunate in this regard; their peer group values do not last for a generation and are rarely stable over a year. Usually, the young person, following the example of his parents, charts his identity by the mores of his contemporaries; these behavior patterns and fads are as shifting as the sand, so the person never knows who he is. It is little wonder that he tires of shifting his identity with the scene and "cops out" with drugs or other escapes.

What is the solution to such a dilemma? It is certain that it will not be resolved by convincing or coercing one generation to adopt the values of the other, nor should it be. Each is faced with the same basic problem—that of finding an identity which is not based on fluctuating values and circumstances. God has provided for this in the person of Jesus Christ. However, even most of those who have established a personal relationship with the Lord Jesus Christ have never gone on to realize their *identification with him*. This is more than identifying with some church, group, or denomination. Such organizations are made up of people who are encountering the changing faces of our world. And the churches are not exempt from this. Some churches which have changed little for years or even centuries have gone through convulsive changes, even in the past fifteen years. Those who were only identified with a known creed or dogma now find themselves not knowing what their church is, nor who they are. The organized church has traditionally been the last bastion against change, and a quick survey of the turmoil in almost all denominations proves that it has fallen prey to these unsettled conditions. Institutionally, the church does not present a united front nor do its members exhibit a consistency of living. God's power in the miraculous is seldom seen. So the stage has been amply set for young people to reject the organized church as irrelevant. In such a degraded condition it *is* all but irrelevant! However, this is not the true church in the form instituted by the Lord Jesus Christ; it is merely a caricature of it. Those young people who are rejecting a caricature of Christianity haven't the remotest understanding of what orthodox evangelical Christianity really is. Again, their parents have been guilty of making a local church a convenience, a social situation, or a welfare project instead of letting it foster a vital, functional relationship with the living God.

The identity crisis can only be resolved by a discovery of personal identification with the Lord Jesus Christ "who is the same yesterday, today, and forever" (Hebrews 13:8). Our identity in him is unshakable and unchangeable whether it be from generation to generation, century to century or culture to culture. In this, and in no other way, can we have an identity that is independent of circumstances and functional in all of life's relationships.

The Silent Majority

All persons who have entered into a personal relationship with God through the Lord Jesus Christ should be experiencing miracles in their own lives and should be leading other persons into the same supernatural life. Sad to say, this is not the case. Approximately ninety percent of all Christians have never led another person to Jesus Christ. Of those who have, probably ninety-five percent or more have never led another Christian beyond the initial conversion experience into the victorious life.

The vast majority of Christians cannot be distinguished from non-Christians if judged by their daily lives; most would have to be termed "silent" Christians. The emphasis on the temporal or materialistic is so prevalent that total surrender and dependence upon God for all of life's needs is foreign to most Christians.

When their nominal Christianity is not sufficient to meet the vicissitudes of life, psychological symptoms develop and this "silent majority" along with their non-Christian friends require—

Therapy

To summarize the foregoing, both the pleasure-mad throng and the mad-pleasure throng are equally ineffective in meeting their own needs. As a result there comes a day of reckoning, or moment of truth, when the mind and emotions can no longer tolerate substitutes for God.

Typically, the symptoms in the mind and emotions are mistakenly diagnosed as "mental illness," and the ceaseless rounds of the psychologists and psychiatrists begin in another vain attempt to meet their needs without God. Since everyone is doing it from Establishment member to subculture dropout, mental health has become like motherhood, although much less understood.

As the problem of mental health becomes an enigma which everyone recognizes and many talk about, there is frenzied activity, enormous outlay of money, and a paucity of results. It seems that in this field persons will tolerate little or no return for their money and go back for more with many getting worse all the while.

Hans J. Eysenck has done considerable research relative to the results of psychotherapy. An article entitled "The Inefficacy of Therapeutic Processes with Adults" appears in the book, *Sources of Gain in Counseling and Psychotherapy*, edited by Bernard G. Berenson and Robert R. Carkhuff. This article was a report covering the results of nineteen studies reported in the literature, describing over 7000 cases, and dealing with both psychoanalytic and eclectic types of treatment. Eysenck's conclusions are:

[25]

In general, certain conclusions are possible from these data. They fail to prove that psychotherapy, Freudian or otherwise, facilitates the recovery of neurotic patients. They show that roughly two-thirds of a group of neurotic patients will recover or improve to a marked extent within about two years of the onset of their illness, whether they are treated by means of psychotherapy or not.

Despite the mounting evidence to the contrary and frank questioning within the ranks of psychotherapists as to the efficacy of their work, their offices are filled with those seeking bread but who are being handed (or thrown) stones.

As the author has discovered, it is not popular to oppose traditional psychiatry and psychotherapy and to posit a spiritual transformation as the *only* solution—not an adjunct, complement, or supplement. This is, however, *the thesis of this book;* and it is supported by empirical evidence, proving that where psychotherapy has either failed completely or caused harmful results in many lives, the person subsequently has been healed through Spirituotherapy at GFI. It is ironic that ministers are sometimes less receptive than psychotherapists to such a claim. Debunking psychotherapy seems to be akin to maligning God—even in Christian circles. Though the bulk of psychotherapy has its roots in Freud's godless (and frequently groundless) principles of psychoanalysis, Christians persist in attempting to build on this foundation of shifting sand an anomaly called, "Christian psychotherapy." It is the position of the author that these two words are antithetical and mutually exclusive.

Nonetheless, there are many Christians within the ranks of psychotherapists who are sound in their faith and fundamental in doctrine. They do much to alleviate suffering on the part of emotionally disturbed patients and many return to a fuller life who are much better adjusted psychologically.

This apparent success is very deceptive, and good psychological adjustment in a Christian is many times mistaken for spiritual maturity. The person may be active in Christian work, even in the ministry, and yet be out of adjustment spiritually. Psychotherapy helps a person to meet his own needs, to learn more effective ways of behavior and to develop more adequate defense mechanisms. In other words, the therapist is saying, "You can do it, Self. You get stronger so you can handle the stresses of life." Conversely, God says in John 15:5, "Without me, you can do nothing." As self (or as Freud would put it, the ego) grows progressively stronger, there is correspondingly less dependence on God; as long as *we* can do it, we will keep trying and failing! Psychotherapy, then, has as its goal to help a person become stronger and stronger. But God says we must become weaker and weaker that he might become our strength (2 Corinthians 12:9). Paul goes on to say in 2 Corinthians 12:10 " ... for when I am weak, then am I strong." Thus, psychotherapy is at cross purposes with God and becomes a substitute for the work of the Holy Spirit. It is one thing to help a person understand the psychodynamics of his behavior; it is entirely another thing to use psychological principles exclusively to attempt behavior change. The underlying principle is that if the behavior is more acceptable, the person will feel better and will be changed in the process. In other words, changing the behavior changes the person. To some degree this is true or therapists would not continue to have a practice. God, however, works on another principle: *change the person, and his behavior will change.* This has been amply proven in conversion experiences, and the change in a Christian's life when he realizes the power of union with Christ may be greater than that experienced at conversion.

Spirituotherapy does not admit of such a condition as "mental illness" since by definition, the problem would be in the mind. It should be pointed out, however, that structural or organic anomalies may exist, such as brain tumor, etc.; these are not generally subsumed under the heading "mental illness," which is functional as opposed to organic in nature. The counselor at GFI works in close correspondence with the medical profession in an effort to recognize and eliminate behavioral difficulties which may be physiological in origin.

Some who are highly respected in the field of mental health are likewise rejecting the notion of "mental illness." Among these are William Glasser, M.D. and Thomas S. Szasz, M.D. Szasz states in the preface to his book *The Myth of Mental Illness* (Harper & Row): "Although mental illness might have been a useful concept in the nineteenth century, today it is scientifically worthless and socially harmful."

In his book, *Reality Therapy* (Harper & Row), Glasser also rejects the concept of mental illness. His basic tenet is that bizarre behavior is merely an ineffective attempt at meeting one's needs, and that a person must meet his needs through another person. In his words from page 8: "At all times in our lives we must have at least one other person who cares about us and whom we care for ourselves. If we do not have this essential person, we will not be able to fulfill our basic needs. One characteristic is essential in the other person: he must be in touch with reality himself and able to fulfill his own needs in the world."

This, too, is the basic premise of Spirituotherapy; the prime difference is that the Person who meets our needs is the Lord Jesus Christ—not a human therapist. If Glasser's book were read with this significant substitution, the approach of Spirituotherapy would be approximated.

While denying that mental aberrations constitute mental illness, both Glasser and Szasz would endorse a type of human therapy.

Though the problem is ultimately spiritual in nature, the obvious manifestation is through mental and behavioral symptoms. O. Hobart Mowrer in his book *The Crisis in Psychiatry and Religion* (© 1961, reprinted by permission of D. Van Nostrand Company) takes a strong stand in favor of a spiritual emphasis in meeting the needs of those who are in emotional and mental distress. His statement from pages 170-171 is: "If religious leaders had been deeply involved in the care and redemption of seriously disturbed persons for the past century, instead of systematically 'referring' such persons, there would have been no Freud and no necessity for a Tillich or a Fosdick to try and legitimize him."

Even though the symptoms are mental and some benefit relative to communication is derived from classification of such symptoms, to attempt therapy in the realm of the psyche or mind is folly since it is merely symptomatic treatment. Some symptoms respond in varying

[29]

degrees to psychotherapy, although the source of the problem is seldom, if ever, touched in the process. In Spirituotherapy there is no benefit in differential diagnosis from a psychological standpoint. This is merely a taxonomy for symptoms. Since the source of the problem is spiritual in nature, it is infinitely more important to determine the spiritual state of the individual. The person rarely cares which particular psychological phenomenon has been his plight, so long as he discovers how to unload it. Some people coming to GFI have been labeled during previous visits to psychotherapists. Some were given little hope for recovery, and others were told outright that they would never be any better.

Through the ministry of GFI, God has delivered persons from many of the symptomatic ailments which now pass for mental illness. Among these are paranoid schizophrenia, obsessive thoughts, several varieties of sex deviation, conversion hysteria, manic depression, reactive depression, sociopathic personality, psychotic reactions, alcoholism, anxiety neurosis, extreme fantasy, and various others.

The counselor in Spirituotherapy is not a therapist but a spiritual guide. The therapy is accomplished by the Master Therapist, the Holy Spirit. Thus, the therapy of the Holy Spirit within the human spirit results in deliverance from psychological symptoms caused by spiritual maladjustment. This is not to say that all psychological difficulties have a spiritual genesis. Many, if not most, of these stem from early childhood, and psychology is beneficial in understanding some of the resultant behavior. However, the use of psychology should stop with understanding. Attempting psychological treatment or psychotherapy is an exercise in futility. For the person who is unwilling to have, or is unaware of, God's answer to his dilemma, psychotherapy is his only recourse for symptomatic relief. But it is not *the* answer.

God did not promise to meet our emotional and mental needs through a counselor, psychologist, or psychiatrist just as he did not promise to meet our visceral or physiological needs through a physician; he did say, "But my God shall supply all your need according to his riches in glory by Christ Jesus" (Philippians 4:19). Spirituotherapy takes Paul's position literally, unequivocally, and unapologetically and trusts God to honor his Word and perform a miraculous deliverance in the life of each person who comes for counseling.

The author voluntarily left a well paid position in the aerospace industry after nineteen years in response to a call from God, knowing that his temporal as well as eternal existence depended upon the promise of God: "Faithful is he that calleth you who also will do it" (1 Thessalonians 5:24). The work was not and is not subsidized by any denomination or group. If the counselor is to be able to tell a person with any degree of conviction that God will supply all of his needs, then the counselor must provide the example by casting himself completely upon the Lord even in the matter of salary. The commitment of the counselor must pervade every area of his life if he is to be a guide and example to those with whom he shares Christ. This is in direct contrast to that of conventional psychotherapy. In many forms of therapy the therapist is not required to have experienced what he prescribes. Records are replete with cases where the therapist is unable to meet his own needs in the world, and this is reflected in his therapy and many times in his family.

The statistics on suicides indicate that the profession of psychiatry has the highest suicide rate of any profession—mute evidence of the failure of the therapeutic climate to meet the deepest needs of the individual—client or therapist. It is a private joke among psychiatrists that the only difference between them and their clients is that they understand and accept their neuroses. The object of the therapy is not to eliminate the source of the neuroses, but to teach better modes of behavior and more adequate defense mechanisms—in other words, *learn to cope with the problem!*

God's purpose in sending the Lord Jesus Christ was not merely to forgive our sins and help us live with our problems by harnessing the old nature to "work for him." The Savior came not only to reconcile us to himself, but to save us *from* ourselves by his life (Romans 5:10). He came to give us life "more abundantly" (John 10:10). It is estimated that more than ninety percent of all Christians never experience the abundant or victorious life, so they do not understand how deep psychological problems can be resolved without human therapy by letting the Lord Jesus Christ manifest his life in them. This same rationale also obtains in the case of many pastors, Christian psychologists, and psychiatrists. Though Christian in their orientation to life, they resort to therapy as a means of showing people how needs can be met.

Most Christian psychologists and psychiatrists are like a Christian carpenter— he drives a nail pretty much like a non-Christian carpenter. This is not to say that a Christian who does therapy is insincere either in his therapy or in his relationship with the Lord Jesus Christ; it is to say that he either has not experienced the abundant life or he doesn't know how to share it in a clinical setting. If he did, he would be forced to repudiate most of his technique as being of questionable value at best and cease *his* therapy in deference to the Holy Spirit's.

It is the thesis of the Word of God and, consequently of Spirituotherapy, that the abundant life and anxiety are mutually exclusive. This is specifically stated in Philippians 4:6, 7: "Be anxious for nothing ... And the peace of God which passeth all understanding shall keep your hearts and minds through Christ Jesus." All Christians enjoy peace *with* God but relatively few enjoy the peace *of* God—the peace that is beyond description and comprehension. It is this peace that the neurotic or psychotic is desperate to know; it is likewise this peace that the so-called well-adjusted person needs even though he does not understand that he *has* a problem until his comfortable world begins to fall apart at the seams. In either case the discipline of adversity (Psalm 119:71) faithfully administered by our loving Sovereign is often necessary before we begin to seek him with all our heart (Jeremiah 29:13). This abundant life or Spirit-filled life is not God's portion merely for a chosen few. He intends that all of his children go beyond knowing Christ as Savior and Lord to know him as *Life*.

It is to this end that this book is dedicated. It is not written just to the professional in the fields of theology and the helping professions but to any searching soul who sincerely wants to know the Lord Jesus Christ as his "all, and in all" (Colossians 3:11).

Why not ask him to search your heart (Psalm

139:23, 24) as you objectively assess your relationship to God in the light of his Word and his power as illustrated in the following chapters? An entirely new life is available to you, even though you may have been a Christian for years, as you yield entirely to that Blessed One who desires to be your life.

Beginning with the next chapter, the material presented is in the order and in much the same manner normally presented to persons as the teaching portion of the counseling interviews. As you read, be willing for God to diagnose your spiritual condition and to "supply all *your* need according to his riches in glory by Christ Jesus" (Philippians 4:19).

ACCEPTANCE

Oh, to know acceptance
In a feeling sort of way;
To be known for what I am—
Not what I do or say.
It's nice to be loved and wanted
For the person I seem to be,
But my heart cries out to be loved
For the person who is really me!

To be able to drop all the fronts
And share with another my fears,
Would bring such relief to my soul,
Though accompanied by many tears.
When I find this can be done
Without the pain of rejection,
Then will my joy be complete
And feelings toward self know correction.

The path to feeling acceptance of God
Is paved with acceptance on Earth;
Being valued by others I love
Enhances my own feeling of worth.
Oh, the release and freedom he gives
As I behold his wonderful face—
As Jesus makes real my acceptance in him,
And I learn the true meaning of grace.

A pity it is that so late we find
His love need not be earned;
As we yield to him all manner of strife
A precious truth has been learned.
Then, as we share with others who search
For love, acceptance, and rest;
They'll find in us the Savior's love.
And experience the end of their quest.

C. R. SOLOMON

HOW SPIRITUOTHERAPY WORKS

If we propose to work with the human being in coping with the problems of living, it is a foregone conclusion that we must understand his basic needs. It is always helpful to have a model or an ideal type to use as a guide in the evaluation of our own lives or in helping others to put the entire picture into proper perspective. Many have attempted this in years past with most of the best developed models leaving little or no room for the spiritual nature of man. One of the most influential in this regard in the past century has been Freud with his psychoanalytic theory. It is suggested that he took the basics for his theory of personality from the Bible, just as we do at GFI. However, he perverted them, while we employ them just as given. His constructs of id, ego, and superego are roughly equivalent to those presented in the Word of God as body, soul, and spirit, respectively. Freud found it necessary to explain the existence, nature, intrapersonal, and interpersonal relationships of man without reference to Deity. To deny the genius of Freud in developing a counterfeit system in rivalry to God would be to show a complete lack of understanding of the monumental work that he did. Also, to refuse to profit by his research and understanding of human behavior would be to ignore a great body of knowledge which is extremely useful, providing it is used solely for understanding and *never* for therapy.

We have developed the wheel illustration to

[37]

depict the interrelationships of body, soul, and spirit and have proven in a clinical setting that God's constructs are adequate to explain the totality of human behavior. You will note that some of the terms developed by Freud and his successors to define certain behavioral traits are utilized when appropriate, since these terms are well understood and afford a means of communication. Persons who come for counseling are not given a label such as *schizophrenic* even when it is recognized that their symptoms might fit such a category. Such a label is really unnecessary since Christ is the cure for every emotional ill.

As you will note on the illustration, the *soul* might be called our self-consciousness or the vehicle through which we relate to others, actually our psychological makeup. The *spirit* is our God-consciousness or the facet of our makeup by which we relate to God. The *body*, of course, is the means by which we relate to the world or our environment through our five senses. In summary, we relate to others through our soul, to God through our spirit, and to our environment through our body. The soul is composed of the mind or intellect, the emotions or affections, and the will or volition. Similarly, the *spirit* has the functions of intuition, conscience, and communion. (See *What is Man?* by T. Austin-Sparks.)

As depicted by the arrow between body and soul, there can be physical problems such as an endocrine imbalance or other ailments which can have an adverse effect on our emotional state. Likewise, we can suffer from long-standing psychological symptoms which affect our spiritual life and hamper our walk with God. Being spiritually maladjusted will produce or

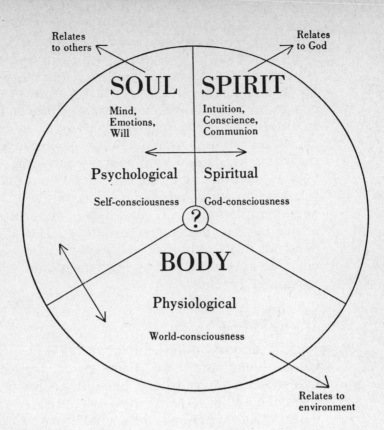

Relates
to others

Relates
to God

SOUL | SPIRIT

Mind,
Emotions,
Will

Intuition,
Conscience,
Communion

Psychological   Spiritual

Self-consciousness   God-consciousness

?

BODY

Physiological

World-consciousness

Relates to
environment

Man—a tri-unity

DIAGRAM 1

amplify existing psychological symptoms. So, we can have difficulties in any of the three areas which may in turn have an adverse effect on another area. It will be necessary to refer constantly to the wheel diagram as we proceed to differentiate the functions of body, soul, and spirit and the understandings we should have regarding needs and problems in each area. Of course, the first and prime consideration is our relationship with God. Unless and until a personal relationship is established, the content of this book is just so much rhetoric. That personal relationship and its necessary concomitants are listed under "spirit" and are explained as follows:

1. Salvation:

This is variously defined as conversion to Christ, being born again, being saved, trusting Christ as Savior and Lord, accepting Christ, receiving Christ, coming to know Christ, entering into a personal relationship with God through personal faith in Jesus Christ. Unless the Lord Jesus Christ is *in* our life he cannot make the necessary changes. His entrance into the life brings about a spiritual birth which is only the beginning of our life in Christ. Before we trust the Lord Jesus Christ in a personal surrender, the Holy Spirit must convince us that we are *born* sinners.

Romans 5:12 concludes, "Wherefore, as by one man [Adam] sin entered into the world, and death by sin; and so death passed upon *all* men, for that all have sinned." Since we are born with a sinful nature, we naturally commit sins. According to Romans 3:23, "All have sinned and come short of the glory of God."

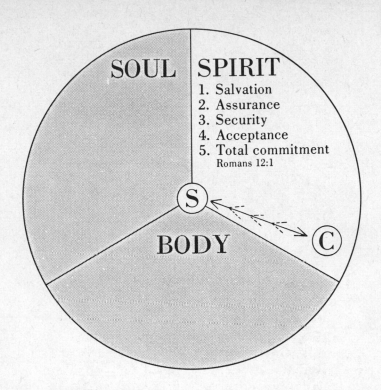

DIAGRAM 2

The penalty for the sin is given in Romans 6:23: "For the wages of sin is death; but the gift of God is eternal life through Jesus Christ our Lord." The death penalty must be paid, and it has been paid: "But God commendeth [shows] his love toward us, in that, while we were yet sinners, Christ died for us" (Romans 5:8).

When we are ready to admit that we are ungodly and believe on the Lord Jesus Christ, then we will be justified or counted righteous in God's sight. "But to him that worketh not, but believeth on him that justifieth the ungodly, his faith is counted for righteousness" (Romans 4:5). The method is very simple: we merely believe what the Bible says about us (we are ungodly sinners), and we also believe what the Bible says about the Lord Jesus (that he was and is God, that he died for our sins, and that he rose from the dead). This is very clearly stated in Romans 10:9, 10: "That if thou shalt confess with thy mouth the Lord Jesus, and shalt believe in thine heart that God hath raised him from the dead, thou shalt be saved. For with the heart man believeth unto righteousness, and with the mouth confession is made unto salvation."

After we hear and believe we must call upon God in prayer: "For whosoever shall call upon the name of the Lord shall be saved" (Romans 10:13). A prayer this simple will do: Dear God, I know I am a sinner. I believe that you sent your Son, the Lord Jesus Christ to die for my sins, that he was buried and that he rose from the dead. I surrender now and turn from a life of sin and trust the Lord Jesus Christ to forgive my sins and to be my Life. Thank you for saving me for Jesus' sake. Amen.

Upon the basis of his infallible Word he saves us when we believe and call upon him. After we have settled the question of salvation in our lives, we can rejoice in—

2. *Assurance:*

It is possible to be saved but not be assured of that salvation. Our assurance must be based on the facts of Scripture rather than on fluctuating feelings. The neurotic most often wants to feel something rather than believe it, and his style of living is to distort reality. As a result there is no reason for him to believe that his feelings will be trustworthy in the matter of salvation. We have run across persons in counseling, Christians for up to forty years, who assumed they were not saved because of the defeated lives they had been living. Their feelings did not witness to the fact that the Lord Jesus Christ was an abiding reality in their lives. One such person had been a victim of obsessive thoughts for eighteen years for which he had received psychotherapy and electroshock therapy in an institution as well as some private psychotherapy. When God delivered him, it became obvious that it had been a spiritual problem all along. He had not been certain of his position in Christ and therefore could not trust God to meet all his needs. Many deep-seated psychological symptoms have their roots in a defective understanding of an existing relationship with God. Many persons proceed in the order of feelings, faith, fact. They should instead proceed according to the facts as God has revealed them in his Word, then faith in these facts, and finally, allow their feelings to be guided by faith in God's facts. The Bible (1 John 5:11-13) tells us that we are to *know* that we have eternal life. It is not at all presumptuous to take God at his Word and simply rest in it. We can establish our assurance only by accepting God's Word for what it is.

Then we must go on to realize that we have—

3. Security:

Our relationship with him is unbreakable—eternal. We are secure in that relationship, and we cannot have assurance if we are not secure and confident that this relationship is lasting. Colossians 3:3 tells us that our "life is hid with Christ in God." If we do not realize this, our assurance cannot be solid because we are afraid we will lose our salvation. And if we are afraid we will lose it, we will struggle to do something in order to maintain it, such as good works. As a result, we cease to live by grace and begin to live again by the law. This is falling from grace into a legalistic condition (Galatians 5:4). This is the condition of many evangelical Christians; they are saved by grace, but bound by the law. At least this is the practical outworking of their insufficient knowledge. Unless a person has his security nailed down, he will not mature in his relationship with Jesus Christ. Of course, assurance and security really go hand in hand. You cannot experience one in any degree without the other.

Then, the fourth thing we need to realize is the fact of

4. Acceptance:

Some accept the Lord Jesus Christ as personal Savior and Lord and then spend the rest of their lives trying to get him to accept them. Of course, this is wheel spinning, because Ephesians 1:6 assures us that "we are accepted in the beloved." Our acceptance doesn't depend on our good works, or how much we read the Bible, or how much we go to church, or any other effort we may expend. *Salvation is grace from start to finish.* Acceptance is by grace, too. God accepts his Son; and since we are in his Son ("accepted *in* the beloved"), he accepts us as well.

Many today have difficulty believing that their parents accept them, or that their peers accept them. In fact, many persons feel that *no one* really accepts them. As a result, they come to feel that God does likewise; if they are not fit for other people to accept, why should God accept them? Of course, this isn't the case. But if a person *feels* that way, to him this sense of rejection is real. And what is the answer? He must come to the place where he realizes he is accepted. He *is* acceptable, not because of anything he has done, but because of the great things the Lord Jesus Christ has done. When he was saved—when he trusted the Lord Jesus as his personal Savior—he was put *into* Christ (1 Corinthians 1:30). Being put into Christ, he is accepted by God *in Christ*. In this, as in the initial salvation experience, we must take God at his Word and believe what he says regardless of how we feel about it. As we begin to take him at his Word, our feelings start to line up with the facts.

Acceptance by God and identification with Christ in death, burial, and resurrection are much like opposite sides of a coin. When one is realized in experience, the other will be also. A case in point is that of a woman who had been filled with extreme hostility. She had tried psychiatry to no avail before coming to Grace Fellowship. After approximately three counseling interviews and attendance at three lectures by the author, God delivered her in the following manner. She had intellectually

[45]

understood the principles set forth in this book, when on Saturday night she began to meditate on Galatians 2:20: "I am crucified with Christ..." On Sunday morning as she was driving to church she was singing the hymn, "Calvary Love." As she sang the refrain, "I long to be worthy of Calvary love," the Holy Spirit dealt with her. She realized that *in Christ* she *was* worthy. She began to weep and cry out, "I *am* accepted; I am *acceptable*." The question of her acceptance was settled as was the extreme hostility. No longer was she troubled with psychological difficulties which had beset her since childhood.

The fifth item under *spirit* is:

5. *Total commitment:*

Consecration, dedication, surrender, submission, and other terms are used to denote this vital step in the Christian's life. It is necessary to define the term as we will be using it in this book. Romans 12:1 tells us, "I beseech you therefore, brethren, by the mercies of God, that ye present your bodies a living sacrifice, holy, acceptable unto God, which is your reasonable service." Total commitment according to this verse is something *we* can do; it is *our* "reasonable service." It is an act of the will, where we tell our Father that we want more than anything else in this world to have his will accomplished in our lives, whatever that means. We don't know his specific purpose in this life for us; but after we have wholly committed our lives to him, he begins to bring it to pass (Psalm 37:5).

Total surrender is essential to total usefulness. Occasionally a person accepts the Lord Jesus Christ as Savior and makes him Lord of his life at the beginning. This is what should happen in all conversions! One should not accept Jesus Christ as Savior and then wait ten or fifteen years to yield completely to him. This should all happen the day a person accepts Christ. When it doesn't, a person has to see the futility of running his own life (or ruining it, as is frequently the case) and come to the place where he is ready to say, "Lord, I want to take my hands off my life; I want you to run it." This decision is comparable to the marriage ceremony where a man and a woman are joined in holy matrimony. Each of them says by an act of the will, "I do." Based upon this act of their wills, before God and a minister, they are pronounced man and wife. They have met the legal requirements for marriage. The act of the will has been made, but the woman still is not a wife until the marriage union is consummated. With an act of the will they have made a decision which changes the entire course of their lives. But neither of them feels automatically like a wife or a husband. The total commitment to the Lord is much the same, where by an act of our will we say, "I do" or "I will." "Whatever you want, your will be done in my life."

Our wills have been exercised, but as a usual rule we are not miraculously transformed at that time, although some persons are. A few who come for counseling are at the point where there is no way out. When they come through in a complete surrender, God consummates the transformation in the life immediately or in a very short time. But in most cases, once this surrender is made, with or without emotion, there is little observable change. From that point, the responsibility is turned over to God and he begins to bring about a consummation of his purpose and plan in that life. His first step is to consummate the relationship by getting *us* out of the way! This will be further explained shortly.

Looking back to Romans 12:1, we surrender our lives as "a living sacrifice." This hearkens back to the Old Testament sacrifice where the lamb was put on the altar. That lamb, though, had no choice; someone else put him there. As he was bound on the altar, he was totally committed. He could not say to the priests, "Now, listen, do anything to me, but don't cut my throat!" This was exactly what they had in mind. The lamb was totally under the control of another. There were no reservations that he could make. And, this is exactly what our surrender must be if our faithful High Priest is to bring about the consummation in our lives where we will experience the fullness of our union with Jesus Christ.

In the salvation experience referred to in item 1, where we invite Christ into our lives, he comes into our spirit. This is represented by the "C" down in the lower part of the diagram. Christ is in the life, but he can be *in* the life without being the *center* of the life. Tragically, this is true of most Christians. In fact, usually a person is so busy with life, and the wheel of life is spinning so rapidly, that Christ is forced to the periphery of the life by a process similar to centrifugal force. It may be, too, that a person is so busy working *for* the Lord that he doesn't have time to spend *with* him. As a result, Christ is not central in the life. But in the trials and adversities that God permits in our lives, this wheel of life can slow down. Many times God permits it to come to a screeching halt. Then Christ can begin to move toward the center of the life (see arrow). But if Christ is not the center of our

[48]

lives, something else is. The thing or person that is so important that it becomes the motivating force of our lives is referred to as the center of the life.

The S in the center of the circle might, for instance, represent *some thing* such as a home, or a car, or some other thing that we feel would really make us happy. Usually, we strive and struggle to get these things, and once the newness wears off, we find we have won a hollow victory. Or, instead of some thing, it might be *some person* at the center of our life. This person might be a father, a mother, a husband, a wife, a child, a boyfriend, or a girlfriend—some person in our lives we seek to please or satisfy so that we can feel good about ourselves. This might be either a positive or a negative orientation. For instance, one or both of our parents could cause us to feel a certain way about ourselves so that, even though they might be hundreds of miles away, or deceased, we still feel about ourselves the way they caused us to feel. To all intents and purposes, they are still inside; our life is oriented around them.

It might be *success* (however we define that in our own lives). It might be a businessman struggling to get to the top, to become the president of the company. A minister may seek success by struggling to work, work, work to get to a place where he can have a more influential ministry or a bigger church. For a student it might be making straight "A's." Whatever the way, the motivating force in life is achieving success.

For a sex deviate, it might be that *sex* is the most important thing in his life; his life is centered around sex. It might be *drugs* and the experience to be derived from them. A heroin addict might consider that the most important thing in his life is getting another fix, and this becomes his all-consuming passion. If he has enough drugs, he feels that everything is fine. Or, it could be *money* and the things dollars buy; material things are all important to many. But all of these manifestations represent things *we* want or something that *we* think will give *us* great satisfaction. All of these S's may be summed up in the term *self* (or flesh).

Self may be defined as all that we are outside of the Lord Jesus Christ or as Scripture terms it, *flesh*. Someone has said we can drop the *h* from *flesh* and spell it backwards and we have *self*. This is not to be confused with the psychological self or soul—the mind, emotions, and will—which causes us to be a unique individual. The soul, in and of itself, is neutral; it is the driving force which empowers the soul that determines the attitudes and actions and their ultimate worth. Self at the center of the life means *we* are in control or at least trying to be. Of course, no one is able by himself to control his life. We were designed so that if we will give volitional consent, God will control our spirit, our spirit will control our soul, and our soul will control our body. This is God's plan, and for it to work, Christ must be at the control center. We should be Christ-centered rather than self-centered. But the majority of Christians, even those in full-time Christian service who are doing much work for the Lord, find that they are still doing it *for* him.

Hudson Taylor is a typical example of this. As a young person he was saved and called into the ministry. After preparation he went to the mission field and was used of God to found the China Inland Mission. He went out completely in faith, totally dependent upon God to supply every need, financial and otherwise. God blessed Hudson Taylor's work and sent out many missionaries who also had to be completely dependent on God. But Taylor was on the mission field between ten and fifteen years before he finally came to the end of Hudson Taylor and all his own resources and quit trying to work *for* God. Then Christ began to live and work *through* him. This is well-detailed in a book entitled *Hudson Taylor's Spiritual Secret.* Even though this man of God accomplished much, it was Hudson Taylor doing it for God until he allowed God to do it through him.

God does not want us to work *for* him, to witness *for* him, to live *for* him. He wants to get self out of the way so he can work through us. This is the lesson that most Christians never learn. Usually it is only learned through hardship, trial, affliction, and suffering to the point where self is dealt with. Self, then, is no longer the center of our life. Our mind and emotions are controlled by the indwelling Christ as we will or reckon upon our resources in him. Until this process is completed, self is in control and we use our own will and mind to run our lives instead of only using them in the doing role. As a result, we are less effective in living. If God is running our lives, then our mind, emotions and will are free to serve his purposes unhampered by the additional duties of trying to decide how we should live our life. As long as self is in control, the functions of the soul will be in direct correspondence to the historical events which have characterized our maturation.

Looking now at the psychological (or "Soul") functions, we will consider some needs and difficulties a person may face. First of all, let's

[51]

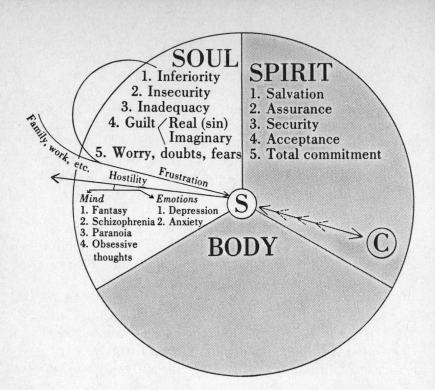

DIAGRAM 3

consider the item called *inferiority*. This plagues many if not most people to some extent. With some persons, feelings of inferiority are so intense that their relationships with other people are hampered. It can hinder their work to the point that when assignments are given to them, they have to fight to get to the place, finally, where they can begin the task. Once they get started, they usually do an exceptional job; but they still feel they cannot achieve. Their minds tell them one thing, and their feelings tell them another. Usually, they know intellectually that they are not inferior; but they *feel* that they are. This causes some serious emotional problems, because a person must compensate for it in some way.

The next item is *insecurity*. This is being filled with fears and doubts about ourselves or what is going to happen next, or always contending with the feeling that something terrible is bound to come up. We cannot relax and have that good feeling inside because of the apprehension which in turn spawns other symptoms. Insecurity in the marriage relationship gives rise to jealousy, and jealousy to accusations; and the cycle often goes on until divorce results. Insecurity in the work relationship causes persons to be afraid they will lose their job or be demoted, and this causes them to be ineffective.

Number three is *inadequacy*. This can take two forms—the form of personal inadequacy, or of feeling inadequate in certain situations. Personal inadequacy is the idea again of feeling inferior—in almost any situation, totally inadequate to cope with life. But some people only feel inadequate in certain situations. For instance, a person might feel inadequate in his

[53]

home, in a family role; but he might feel totally adequate on the job. He might be a professional man, or an executive in a company; and in his work he is held in esteem. He is admired, so he feels wonderful and stays overtime, possibly working ten or twelve hours a day since he is comfortable in that situation. In the home relationship, he cannot get along with his wife or his children, so he stays at work and becomes a loyal company man. It's not because he likes the work so much, but because he cannot make it at home. The converse could be true, where a person feels protected and safe at home; but he is afraid to go on the job because he is really not making a success of it.

Fourth, the ugly specter of *guilt* rears its head. Two kinds of guilt need to be considered. The first is *real guilt,* and we must face it as such. We must not try to explain it away or cover it and call it "guilt feelings," but show it to be the result of sin just as the Word of God proclaims it. The only cure for real guilt and its cause, sin, is the blood of Jesus Christ. First John 1:9 promises, "If we confess our sins, he is faithful and just to forgive us our sins, and to cleanse us from all unrighteousness." This is the only way real guilt can be expiated or put away. Of course, all sin and guilt is dealt with when we are saved, when we trust Jesus Christ, but afterward the sin that crops up in our lives must be dealt with by acknowledging it to God and forsaking it. If we do this, he forgives and cleanses.

In addition to the real guilt which all of us have, many also have *imaginary guilt.* This feels like real guilt. We can confess, and confess, and confess, and still be plagued with the problem. Many persons think because of this, they have committed the unpardonable sin, or that there is some sin that they just cannot uncover. They do not know what it is. They feel that if they could find it and confess it, they would be free. Imaginary guilt may spring from a lack of love and acceptance. As an unwanted child, a person may feel no deep sense of belonging. Sometimes he is told that he is unwanted and sometimes he merely senses it. As a result, he becomes conscience-smitten for being there; he feels he is causing all the problems. If he were out of the picture, the family would be fine. He feels guilty for being there and grows up feeling guilty for even being a person. This imagined guilt persists throughout life. Understanding imaginary guilt is the first step in turning it over to the Lord; experiencing God's acceptance is the antidote to rejection.

Lastly, we will consider the general category of *worry*, *doubts*, and *fears*. When we have inner turmoil, we are prone to worry. God's Word admonishes us to be anxious for nothing (Philippians 4:6). But most people ignore that and worry about everything. When we do, we have various doubts—doubts that other people love us or doubts that God is real. We may doubt that he will meet our needs, and so we begin to fret. Nagging doubts cause many kinds of fears. It can be fear of failure; it can be any of a myriad of fears. Fear is all-pervasive, and it can really wreck us and our testimony. It can become irrational, and then it is called a phobia. The underlying cause of every phobia is a faulty faith. In fact, the five preceding symptoms are indicative of a failure to trust in and depend fully upon the Lord though we may have known him as Savior and even as Lord for years.

When we have all these things going on inside

and acting upon each other, inner turmoil results. The internal frustration is compounded by external stresses from family, work, and other adverse conditions. You will note on the wheel that we have encircled all five items and labeled the result as frustration. This frustration has a direct bearing on self. The result can be illustrated by the striking of a golf ball. If the ball has a live center, it will react with the club head and travel a great distance. If the center is dead, not much is going to happen. If self is very much alive and the frustration comes in, then the automatic result is hostility. If we strike our hand on something and knock the skin off, we do not have to think very much before we get upset and want to throw something. The problem is, how are we going to handle that hostility? One of the prime goals of the psychotherapist is to teach a person how to handle hostility. This is futile because as soon as you learn how to handle it, it is going to pop up in another form. The problem is not how to handle it, but how to prevent it! The hostility is sometimes projected onto someone else (displaced hostility), usually a person who does not deserve it; and we get it out of our system. The pressure is relieved to some extent, but additional guilt is incurred which serves to increase the frustration, and we commit another hostile act. On and on the cycle goes.

Psychotherapy advocates getting out feelings, emotional catharsis, as a means of venting hostility. This is workable in the therapeutic climate, but not all persons have a safe situation in which to dump their hostility. Society at large does not accept negative feelings with tender loving care. Many persons are filled with hostility who have no acceptable means of dealing with it. They cannot verbalize it satisfactorily and they cannot exercise violence toward other people to get it out. They either keep all or some of it inside. When hostility is kept inside, the conflict can travel in either of two directions as shown on the diagram. It can affect our mind or our emotions. If it influences the mind, there are several things that can happen.

One is fantasy: a person can spend his time thinking how he would *like* things to be. A little of this is acceptable because sometimes we do make our daydreams come true. But, if we live in a fantasy world, then we are not effective in the real world. A person who is prone to this, and some who are not, might have a psychotic break and becomes schizophrenic where they live in an unreal world. They are institutionalized and permitted to live in that unreal world because they are incapable of living in reality. Or, they might become paranoid due to a feeling of inadequacy or guilt. A person who feels inadequate usually blames his failures on someone else. This becomes a pattern and he begins to believe his own lie. Eventually, he becomes certain that a person or group is really out to get him. This may also stem from guilt where the person feels a need to be punished. In his fantasy he imagines that individuals or groups intend him bodily harm. Instead of being completely out of touch with reality, he usually has well structured delusions; whereas in other areas of life he is pretty well adjusted. Another trick the mind plays is to be obsessed with certain thoughts of which the person cannot rid himself; he typically performs some act such as washing his hands to get relief. These aberrations are not mental illnesses, but they are mental symptoms of a deeper problem—self at the center of the life. Treating symptoms rarely effects a permanent cure. Persons can go to psychiatrists all of their lives for treatment of such symptoms.

In addition to symptoms in the mind, the frustration can affect the emotions, another area of the soul. Or, both the mind and emotions may be affected. A common effect on the emotions is depression; hostility kept inward becomes depression. We push against ourselves. We take it out on ourselves instead of taking it out on someone else. We beat ourselves severely about the head and shoulders, which causes us to be depressed, anxious, and tied up in knots. This can be simple depression or it can become more severe and be termed reactive depression or manic depression. Still, these are not basically mental problems or real emotional problems, they are symptoms of a deeper problem. The problem is usually treated by attempting to rid the afflicted one of the anxiety and depression which has been bottled up inside.

This anxiety and depression is usually contained until it is no longer possible to keep it inside. Then it manifests itself in the body as a psychosomatic or psychophysiological symptom. Many of these could be listed. It can be a tension headache which can become migraine, or it can be a nervous stomach and the ubiquitous antacid pills and liquids. The nervous stomach is the breeding place for a peptic ulcer. Some other common ailments stemming from psychological conflict are hives, some forms of arthritis, asthma, skin rashes, spastic colon, palpitations of the heart, respiratory ailments, and conversion hysteria,

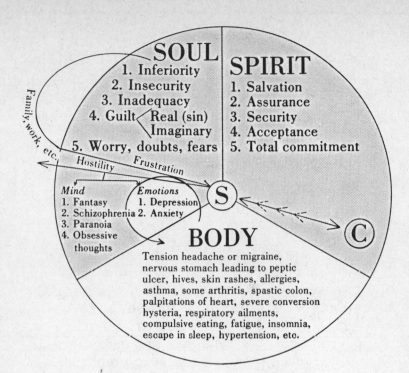

DIAGRAM 4

where emotional conflict is converted into physical symptoms. Some medical doctors estimate that 60 to 80 percent of their patients have ailments caused by emotional and psychological conflict. If a person has "the peace of God which passeth all understanding" (Philippians 4:7) in his life, he cannot have emotional conflict. Ultimately, these physical or psychosomatic symptoms are spiritual problems.

To summarize, it is because self is at the center of the life that all this conflict has developed and continues to grow. The problems may have been there since childhood, but the fact that they continue means that self is running the life. It may be good self, it may be bad self, it may be in-between self; but it is still self, and *self in control of the life is repugnant to God.* In psychotherapy, of whatever persuasion, self is strengthened to cope with those problems. Herein lies the basic problem with psychotherapy. With enough psychotherapy many of the symptoms will respond so that a person becomes better adjusted, with the symptoms either diminishing or leaving. But, in order to cope with them, better defense mechanisms are built and self becomes stronger. Thus, when symptoms improve as a result of psychotherapy the problem, self-centeredness, always gets worse! This is diametrically opposed to what God does, because God's way of dealing with self is that it must become weaker and weaker until its control is finally phased out. Self is reduced to nothing so that Christ can be everything. This is the process by which Christ becomes the center of the life.

When Christ is in control, self, or flesh, no longer holds sway. It is not permanently

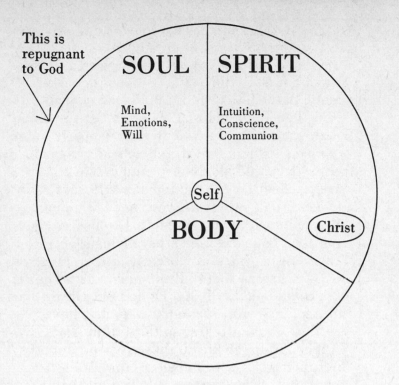

DIAGRAM 5

replaced, but the cross blocks the power of sin as it is reckoned so. We are still a unique self or individual, empowered by the life of Christ within. When Christ is in the center of the life—when Christ is in control of the life—then Philippians 2:5 says, "Let this mind be in you which was also in Christ Jesus." We can have *his* mind or attitudes. Philippians 4:13 says, "I can do all things through Christ which strengtheneth me." Philippians 4:19 says, "But my God shall supply *all* your needs [including the emotional] according to his riches in glory, [not by a counselor, or a psychologist, but] by Christ Jesus." When Christ is at the center of the life, he can meet all the needs as he has free rein to do the living. Of course, Christ does not feel insecure, inadequate, guilty, have worries, doubts, fears; so those things are expelled from the life. If they are gone from the life, then we are no longer a bundle of frustration. If we are not frustrated, then we are not hostile. When the outer stresses occur with Christ at the center, then he doesn't react with hostility but with just the opposite—love, understanding, and compassion. And, then, of course, if there is no frustration and hostility to be kept bottled up inside the life, there is nothing to adversely affect the mind or emotions. The mental and emotional symptoms are purged from the life; and, if all that has caused the conflict inside is gone, the resulting psychosomatic symptoms leave also.

Naturally, if the body has organic damage such as a duodenal ulcer, it takes time for that to heal. But many times, we see instantaneous deliverance from such things as tension headaches, nervous stomach and other pain caused by tension. When the peace of God

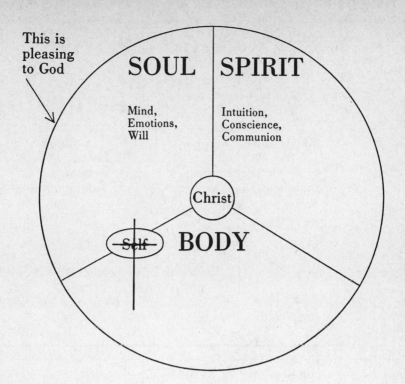

DIAGRAM 6

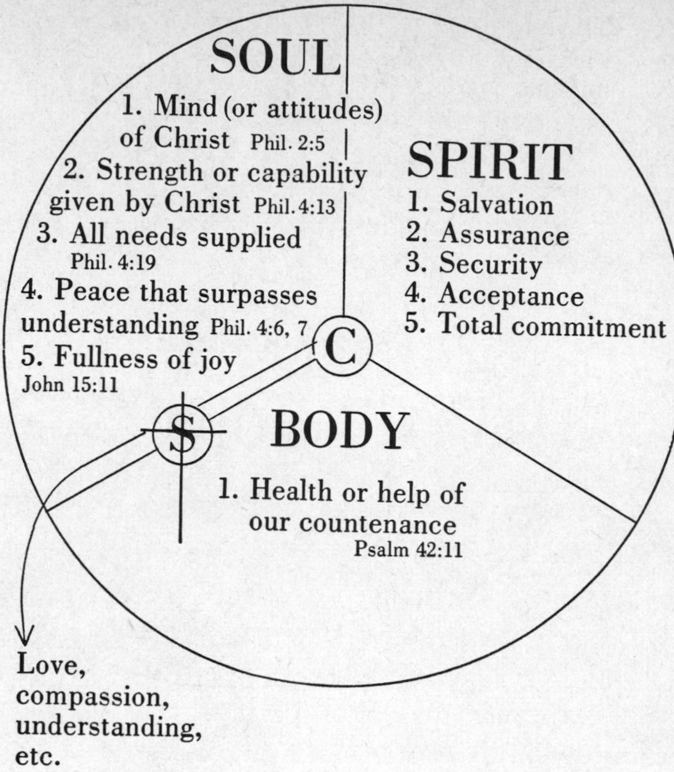

SOUL

1. Mind (or attitudes) of Christ Phil. 2:5
2. Strength or capability given by Christ Phil. 4:13
3. All needs supplied Phil. 4:19
4. Peace that surpasses understanding Phil. 4:6, 7
5. Fullness of joy John 15:11

SPIRIT

1. Salvation
2. Assurance
3. Security
4. Acceptance
5. Total commitment

C

S

BODY

1. Health or help of our countenance Psalm 42:11

Love, compassion, understanding, etc.

DIAGRAM 7

which passes all understanding becomes the rule of the life then these things must go, whether gradually or dramatically.

Now, the logical question is, how does Christ *become* the center of the life? What truth in God's Word explains this to us? In order to grasp this, it is necessary to think through another illustration—the line diagram. The horizontal line with an arrowhead at both ends represents eternal life; and, of course, eternal life has no beginning and no end. Only one Being has eternal life and that is God; so, really, eternal life is Christ's life. At a point in time, and at an appointed time, he came to earth and took on a human body as a baby being Virgin-born in Bethlehem. But the life that he lived in that body is the same life that he has always lived as God. He lived in a human body for about thirty-three years, and then he ended his earthly existence at the cross where he bore our sins. He died, was buried, and rose again; so his life continued.

At a later point in time each of us entered into a physical existence by a physical birth; but, when we are born, we are not in his life. Instead, we are in another existence represented by the line going through our parents, our grandparents and their ancestors all the way back to Adam. That is where our existence really began—in Adam! We were *in him* positionally when he sinned. This is what made us sinners from birth. Romans 5:12 explains, "Wherefore, as by one man sin entered into the world, and death by sin; and so death passed upon all men, for that all have sinned." Therefore, being *in Adam*, when he sinned—we sinned; when he died (spiritually)—we died, so we are all born dead! (Ephesians 2:1).

When we were born, it was only natural that we

would commit sin—we were born with a sinful nature. Romans 3:23 emphasizes, "For all have sinned, and come short of the glory of God." We sinned—consistent with our nature—and our natural progress was downward. The diagram showing the life "in Adam" indicates this downward trend. This is verified by Romans 6:23: "For the wages of sin is death [spiritually and eternally, as well as physically] but the gift of God is eternal life through Jesus Christ, our Lord." Since we are born spiritually dead, our greatest need is life. We received physical life by physical birth and we likewise receive spiritual life by spiritual birth (John 3:3; 1 John 5:11, 12). The transition line depicts the truth propounded in 1 Corinthians 1:30; "But of him [God] are ye in Christ Jesus, who of God is made unto us wisdom, and righteousness, and sanctification, and redemption." We can be taken out of the old Adam life and put into Christ, by the Spirit of God. Once we are *in* Christ, we are in an eternal existence—a life that is not based on time.

We have asked this question of literally hundreds of people. "What is eternal life?" Their first reaction is "Well, it's life that never ends." Of course, this is true; but this is only half of the truth. The other half of the truth is that once we have entered into Jesus Christ, we have an eternal life that spans the past as well as the future.

This new life is traced back—not through our ancestors to Adam—but back through Christ to (and beyond) the cross. Calvary is an event in eternity. Being *in Christ* means being in him eternally—eternally future and eternally past. Our life in Christ is an eternal relationship. We

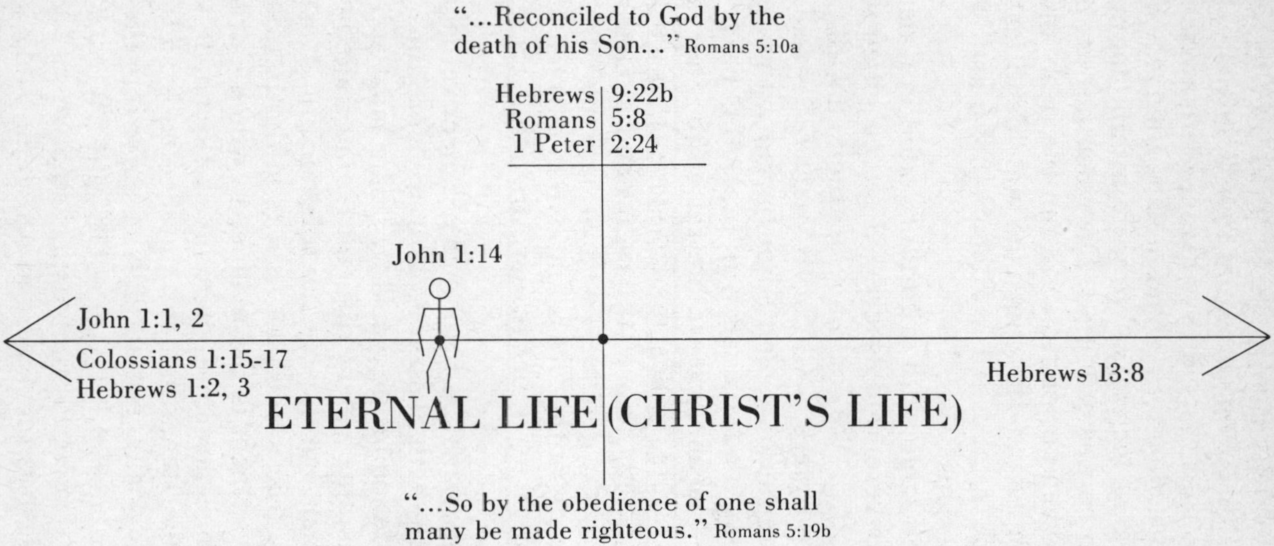

"...Reconciled to God by the death of his Son..." Romans 5:10a

Hebrews 9:22b
Romans 5:8
1 Peter 2:24

John 1:14

Hebrews 13:8

ETERNAL LIFE (CHRIST'S LIFE)

"...So by the obedience of one shall many be made righteous." Romans 5:19b

John 1:1, 2
Colossians 1:15-17
Hebrews 1:2, 3

DIAGRAM 8

are in him presently; we are in him 3000 years in the future; and we are in him 3000 years in the past. Eternity is always present tense since it is not based on time. That means, then, we were in him *at the cross.* We were in him not only when he was crucified, but when he was buried and when he was raised from the dead and ascended into Heaven. This is an identification clearly established in Romans 6:4-6 and Colossians 3:1-3.

The same truth is further stated in Galatians 2:20 where Paul asserts, "I am crucified with Christ...." We could not be crucified with Christ until we were *in* Christ. Romans 6:5 reveals that we are not only planted or buried with him but *raised* from the dead with him. Accepting Christ means that we are raised to a heavenly level of life. Ephesians 2:6 states that we are seated right now at the right hand of God *in* Christ. Ponder this—we can hang up our hang-ups at the Cross and live in Heaven on the way to Heaven, because we are in him there right now!

Ephesians 1:4 turns our perspective back: "... He hath chosen us in him before the foundation of the world...." Like most spiritual truths, this may be difficult for our finite minds to grasp, but this eternal relationship is just as much true in the past as it is in the future.

This, then, is the manner in which Christ becomes the center of our lives. We not only are to understand this truth intellectually and theologically, but actually to enter into the experience of it by an act of faith. We are not referring to some experience where self or the flesh is removed and we obtain sinless perfection; and we are not referring to what is sometimes termed a second work of grace. We

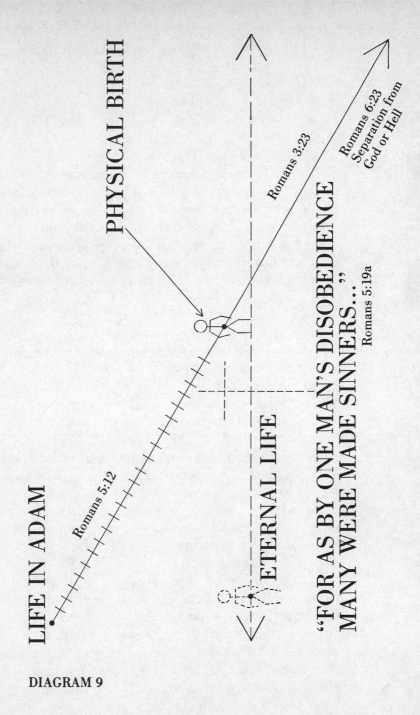

LIFE IN ADAM

PHYSICAL BIRTH

Romans 5:12

Romans 3:23

Romans 6:23
Separation from
God or Hell

"FOR AS BY ONE MAN'S DISOBEDIENCE
MANY WERE MADE SINNERS..."
Romans 5:19a

ETERNAL LIFE

DIAGRAM 9

are talking about entering into something experientially that is already ours positionally —the life of Christ. Though his life is a blessing received the day we are saved, we need to enter into the fullness of Christ, into the Spirit-filled life, into the abundant life or the abiding life, as the Bible variously terms it.

The difference it makes is that we cease trying to live for him and to work for him and to witness for him in the energy of the flesh. Discovering by revelation that we have been crucified and raised to new life, we can now reckon this to be so and let him live and labor through us. But this demands that we come to the end of ourselves and all of our resources. "Not I, but Christ" is the way Paul expressed it in Galatians 2:20.

How can this no-longer-I-but-Christ awareness take place? It happens differently in every life. But in point of time it has to become as much a reality as the day we trusted Jesus Christ to save us. And it is likewise *by faith*. According to Romans 6:11 we have to "reckon" or believe this to be so. "Likewise reckon ye also yourselves to be dead indeed unto sin, but alive unto God through Jesus Christ our Lord."

Reckoning, or counting upon the fact of co-crucifixion and co-resurrection is an act of volitional choice or invoking the will to appropriate that which God's Word states to be true of us in Christ. This is an act or decision of faith identical in all respects to that of trusting Christ as Savior. God's Word states that we are sinners and that the Lord Jesus Christ fully finished the work for our redemption at Calvary; we claimed this by faith in repentance and surrender and were born again. In the same way, God's Word (the same source) indicates

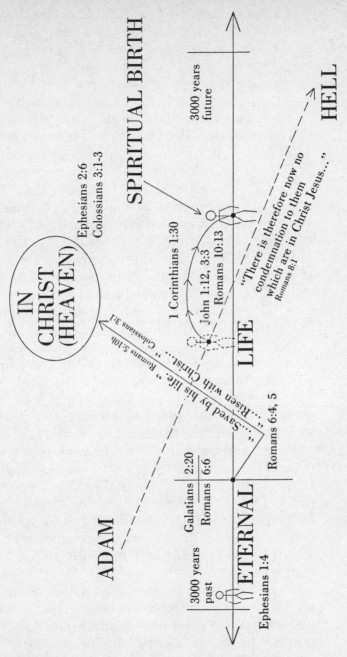

SPIRITUAL BIRTH

Ephesians 2:6
Colossians 3:1-3

3000 years
future

IN
CHRIST
(HEAVEN)

1 Corinthians 1:30

John 1:12, 3:3
Romans 10:13

HELL

"There is therefore now no
condemnation to them
which are in Christ Jesus..."
Romans 8:1

"Saved by his life." Romans 5:10b
"...Risen with Christ..." Colossians 3:1

LIFE

Romans 6:4, 5

ADAM

Galatians 2:20
Romans 6:6

3000 years
past

ETERNAL

Ephesians 1:4

DIAGRAM 10

that we are "self-ers" (controlled by the flesh) and that we participated in his death, burial, resurrection, and ascension, thus freeing us from slavery to sin's power. Again, by volitional choice we appropriate Christ as our Life just as we appropriated Christ as our Savior. In response to our act of faith in appropriating Christ as Savior, the Holy Spirit regenerated us in our spirit; in response to our appropriation of Christ as our Life, the Holy Spirit renews us in our minds (Romans 12:2). The *will* is the vital function since the emotions may be at variance with the facts. As we choose against the world, the flesh, and the Devil and count upon the indwelling Christ to be our life, we are choosing to have our minds and emotions controlled by the Holy Spirit (Ephesians 5:18) such that we can "walk not after the flesh, but after the spirit" (Romans 8:4b) and abide in him (John 15:5).

In some, this has occurred in a gradual way. As they began to understand their position in Christ and his life in them, there was a dramatic transformation. Although this process was gradual, they *knew* that a new awareness of Christ had altered their attitudes in many ways.

We've also seen this identification-realization take the form of a traumatic crisis as God began to make this a vital, living reality. The important thing is not how it takes place, but that we are certain it has happened—that it is now no longer "I," but Christ living and reigning within. This process is described in greater detail in chapter 5.

To reiterate, we must realize that this identification awareness is an event that actually takes place at a point in time and experience. We may not be able to identify that crisis point, the process may be so gradual. But the result is unmistakable—self is dethroned and Christ takes control. This, then, is the way we enter into the Spirit-filled or Spirit-controlled life; we enter in by the way of the cross.

The reality of this does not have to take years and years after conversion. We may realize at the new birth that not only was he crucified *for* us, we were crucified *with* him. It is all true, as far as God is concerned, the day we trust Jesus Christ.

At GFI we sometimes tell people after they accept Jesus Christ as Lord and Savior: "Don't you *ever* try to live the Christian life! You have invited the Lord Jesus Christ into your life, let him live his life in you. That's why he entered your life." And, when we understand this, we see that there is no way we can live a Christian life. It's not a set of rules that we keep; that is legalism. Being enslaved by laws is not freedom (Galatians 5:1). "Ye shall know the truth," Jesus promised, "and the truth shall make you free" (John 8:32). This kind of freedom is inviting Jesus Christ into our life and then letting him live his life in ours. However, it is not a life of passivity but of aggressively yielding our will to his working.

If we are to struggle to live *for* him, then he cannot live *through* us. Until self is dealt with, we continue the self-struggle, perhaps even asking him to help us. We may spend effort and money for him. But this isn't the Christ-centered life. It is simply trying to harness the self life to work for God. During this time of trying, or this trying time, God uses us in spite of ourselves; but he cannot give us the ministry he wants us to have. He cannot multiply and master our ministry to the point where he is doing it through our yieldedness.

It is his goal, his purpose, that we should be conformed to his image (Romans 8:29). If we are going to know this conformity, we have to experience his cross. This is the only way that Christ can become our life initially as well as perpetually. We must let him do the living, so that he can work unhindered through our lives. How this can become a reality is answered by the "Wheel of Life." Are you ready to stop spinning your wheel, so Christ can become your center? If you are, just close your eyes, bow your head, and pray a selfer's prayer. Tell God that you surrender and that he can take over and do whatever he wants with you. Then, claim by faith your death, burial, resurrection, and ascension with Christ and thank God for saving you from yourself, and trust him to live his life through you. "... Yield yourself unto God as those that are alive from the dead, and your members as instruments of righteousness unto God" (Romans 6:13). If the surrender is unconditional, the responsibility for directing the life and the spiritual maturation process has been given to God who has promised, "Faithful is he that calleth you, who also will do it" (1 Thessalonians 5:24). The time and manner of consummation will differ in each life.

THE BACKWARD LOOK

As I mount to view the cross
    From the vantage point of time,
My heart is overwhelmed
    By love and grace sublime.

Sin is ever placed on him (1 Pet. 2:24)
    Who died that I might live; (Rom. 5:10)
Even in his dying throes
    He prayed, "Father, forgive." (Lk. 23:34)

The wonder of forgiveness
    Is a blessing all its own, (Ps. 32:1)
To know that all my guilt
    Has taken wings and flown. (Isa. 6:7)

And then to look to Heaven
    And the bliss I long to know,
It all seems so unreal
    As I struggle here below.

Tho' my heart would do his will (Rom. 7:22)
    With my body his abode, (1 Cor. 3:16)
The flesh resists his call (Rom. 7:18)
    To a high and holy road.

As the turmoil takes its toll,
    And I cry, "Oh wretched man," (Rom. 7:24)
I take a backward look (Heb. 12:2)
    And see redemption's plan.

I had seen the cross as his,
    As the substitute for sin; (Rom. 5:8)
But this was not enough
    To quell the storm within. (Rom. 7:15)

Now the picture comes to me—
    The Spirit's revelation; (Eph. 1:17)
I, too, have been crucified; (Gal. 2:20)
    There is no condemnation! (Rom. 8:1)

The joy of being dead to sin
    And the law which long oppressed, (Rom. 8:2)
Is now my daily portion; (Lk. 9:23)
    I have entered into rest. (Heb. 4:10)

C. R. SOLOMON

WHAT SPIRITUAL MATURITY REALLY MEANS

Spiritual growth or spiritual maturity are terms representing a very vague concept in the minds of most Christians. Many Christians define a "mature" Christian on the basis of the things he does not do, much as a psychologist describes a "normal" person by the absence of symptoms. In other words, a person who is conscientious in observing certain taboos such as drinking and smoking, and who is active in church is considered a "good" Christian.

Another common yardstick for measuring a person's spiritual growth is his prowess as a soul winner—introducing others to the Lord Jesus Christ. Of course, this does represent a degree of growth, and it is proof of new life since we beget after our own kind. However, witnessing or soul winning can be done with self in control of the life, or as the Scripture says, "after the flesh." This is true because most Christians have never experienced the cross and the reality of the Christ-life as presented in the previous chapter.

While spiritual maturity is generally defined in terms of refraining from sinful activities and being involved in Christian service, many times this has little or no spiritual significance and there is no permanent change in life style.

Many a Christian is in a sort of spiritual no-man's land. He has no idea how to proceed in spiritual growth even though he may have the motivation. Since Spirituotherapy is basically counseling for spiritual growth, it is necessary to

[77]

illustrate some guidelines which are valuable in objectively assessing progress in being "conformed to the image of Christ."

These charts present some typical growth patterns in the lives of Christians, and afford the possibility of comparison for the purpose of evaluating our spiritual lives. It is to be understood that the growth patterns are representative of what is; they are not ideal in any sense of the term. It is certainly not God's will that we should go for years or even a lifetime as a spiritual infant or adolescent; it is his desire that we go on to maturity. "Therefore let us go on and get past the elementary stage in the teachings and doctrines of Christ, the Messiah, advancing steadily toward the completeness and perfection that belongs to spiritual maturity ..." (Hebrews 6:1, *Amplified New Testament* © 1958, The Lockman Foundation).

For purposes of comparison, we have also added typical patterns for physical and intellectual maturity.

The horizontal line at the base of the diagram represents our chronological age—our threescore and ten years which we may or may not achieve. The vertical line at the left indicates relative growth or maturity. The upper horizontal line is indicative of the maximum maturity we attain in this life. Of course, this cannot be objectively quantified; and it is different for every individual. For the purpose of clarity in verbally explaining the chart, it is necessary to assign numbers to each of the spiritual patterns.

We will begin with the path depicting the process of physical growth and decline. As represented by the "O," we are usually born at a fairly early age; and we grow rather rapidly for

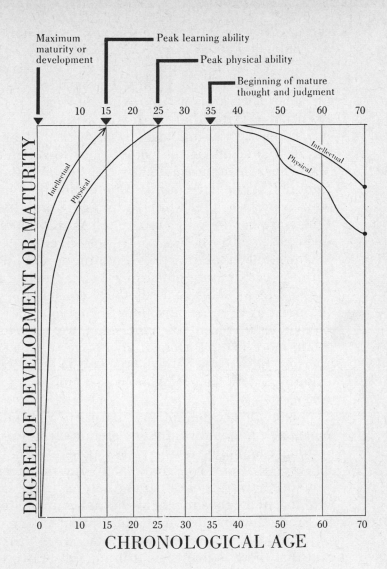

DIAGRAM 11

the first few months. The birth weight should be doubled in about three months and tripled in six. Then, the rate of growth declines, or else we would rapidly become giants. The peak of physical maturity is at approximately age twenty-five. After that there is a gradual declension in physical vigor along with the usual physical ailments as the body begins to wear out. These are represented by the jogs in the right half of the line with the life terminating at age seventy. In other words, after age twenty-five things are bound to get worse unless they have been terribly bad before age twenty-five.

Our intellectual growth is even more rapid, with the peak in rate of learning being reached in the mid-teens. This remains fairly constant through our twenties and then begins to recede. As represented on the chart, we begin to attain more mature thought about age thirty-five since we have made enough mistakes to learn by experience. As we get older, we should get wiser.

If we could chart emotional maturity, we would find that emotional symptoms stemming from youth are amplified as the body begins to lose its reserve of physical stamina. In our younger years we have sufficient strength to maintain our "fronts" or defense mechanisms and continue to be productive in our various life roles. As our physical strength wanes, we are faced with the fact that there is insufficient brain and brawn to fight the battles on the inside and the outside. Our responsibilities may deter us from "copping out" on external activities, but we are increasingly ineffective in maintaining our facade and the emotional symptoms we have had all along become more glaring. This is the reason we see so many in their forties yielding to a

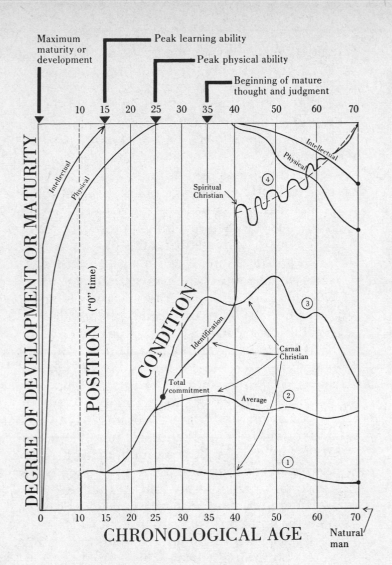

Maximum
maturity or
development

Peak learning ability

Peak physical ability

Beginning of mature
thought and judgment

10 15 20 25 30 35 40 50 60 70

DEGREE OF DEVELOPMENT OR MATURITY

POSITION ("0" time)

CONDITION

Intellectual

Physical

Intellectual

Physical

Spiritual
Christian

④

③

Identification

Carnal
Christian

Total
commitment

Average

②

①

0 10 15 20 25 30 35 40 50 60 70

CHRONOLOGICAL AGE

Natural
man

DIAGRAM 12

variety of neuroses and "nervous breakdowns."
The symptoms can no longer be contained
inside.

Now, let's concentrate on the several lines
representing the spiritual state of man. The
bottom of the chart, the horizontal, depicts the
"natural" man, or the man who has never been
saved from his sinful state. There is,
consequently, no change in his spiritual condition
from birth. He is born estranged or separated
from God and will remain so eternally, unless
he comes to know eternal life in Christ.

The vertical line at age ten represents spiritual
birth or regeneration—conversion. We have
selected this as the average age at which a
person enters into a personal relationship with
the Lord Jesus Christ.

At this point, we must explain two other
concepts—that of *position* and *condition*.
These are often referred to as *standing* and
state. It seems easier to distinguish between the
two by using the former. Looking at the vertical
dotted line from age 10, it continues upward
until it intersects the maximum maturity line at
the top of the diagram. This is to indicate that in
"0" time—immediately and eternally—we are
considered perfect or justified in God's view of
us. This is our *position* as Christians. He sees us
as dead to sin and the law (Romans 8:2) and "alive
unto God through Jesus Christ our Lord"
(Romans 6:11). Our position is perfect since we
have been given a standing in Jesus Christ (1
Corinthians 1:30), and we are presently seated
together "in heavenly places in Christ Jesus"
(Ephesians 2:6).

Though our spiritual *position* is perfect, our
spiritual *condition* may be pathetic! The solid
vertical line at age 10 indicates some initial

change in the life after conversion. But since most ten-year-olds are not gross sinners, there is usually not a great transformation in the life at the time of salvation. Looking to the right at line number one, we see that there is little positive change in the *condition* as time passes. This line represents the person who does not receive sufficient spiritual food (1 Peter 2:2) and goes through life suffering from spiritual malnutrition. Even though he has been brought to life through a spiritual birth, there is no subsequent growth "to be conformed to the image of his Son" (Romans 8:29). In fact, the day he dies he may be in a worse condition than the day he was saved because of the realization that he has wasted his entire life.

Line number two illustrates the average garden-variety Christian. There is a period of little or no growth for a number of years. Some growth begins during the teenage years. It continues as he (or it can just as well be she) takes on the responsibilities of parenthood, including taking the children to church. While the children are growing up, he is active in church and performs some service. God uses him to some extent during this period of time so he feels that he is a "good Christian." When the children leave home, he says to his wife, "Let's let the younger ones do it; we've done our part." He becomes inactive spiritually and begins to coast downhill.

After a number of months or years, he develops a twinge of conscience and decides to try again to be active. For a while the curve turns upward. There is an increase in activity and some growth, but it is still not satisfying so he goes down farther this time. Near the end there is a spurt of effort and spirituality as he crams for his finals! This path represents more defeat than victory even though God honors the effort expended.

The other two lines, numbers three and four, represent Christians who have made a "total commitment" or have completely sold out to Jesus Christ. Line three describes the man who is concerned with his service for Christ. He is a regular bee-hive of activity. He may be an active (or hyperactive) layman or minister who is involved in Christian activity morning, noon, and night. He is generous in his outlays of money as well as time, proving that he has a real burden for the souls of others.

After a good number of years, usually, his defeats begin to outnumber his victories; and he falls back and regroups. He loses ground for awhile and then changes churches or makes some other adjustment and charges ahead again, full bore. He gets a little higher this time, and God may bless his service; but he has farther to fall and does so. He still has not recognized that most of his "accomplishments" are little more than sincere self-effort. So he gathers all his strength for one more gallant try. Failure this time results in the layman dropping out of church or the pastor leaving the ministry. God may bless and use someone who follows such a pattern, in spite of himself, but the person never goes on to spiritual adulthood. It is always some sweet victory along with much defeat. It is an experience-centered life rather than a life of steady growth.

The final path, line four, represents the believer who matures into spiritual adulthood. He, too, has yielded totally to the Lord Jesus Christ, but he is interested primarily in his growth rather than in his service—in *being* rather than *doing*. As a result, he doesn't come on quite as strong as number three, but he is probably used of the Lord as much or more. He goes along at a steady rate of growth for a number of years; and he, too, begins to have problems. He feels that everything is going backwards and that he is bringing reproach on the Lord's name. It may be physical problems, psychological symptoms, tensions with children—these and many other things deplete a believer's self-resources and bring him to the end of himself. He is still going uphill but at a slower pace because he must come to utter helplessness. Only then is he ready for the cross. The chart spots this (the vertical line) at age forty because this is a conservative estimate of the average age at which a Christian enters into the abiding, abundant life of identification with Christ. This is not to say that a person can not appropriate the Christ-life earlier; it is merely a statement of fact about present-day Christianity.

Primarily because of ignorance, identification usually does not become a practical experience for many until years after the life has been totally surrendered to the Lord Jesus Christ. God uses adverse circumstances along with enlightenment in his Word to bring us to the end of our resources. We get so sick of ourselves we can not stand ourselves. Usually only after we have reached this point, does the truth of crucifixion with Christ and life in Christ produce a deep, dramatic transformation. Often the change is much greater than at salvation. When we are saved, the sin is forgiven; but the flesh continues to pump out the sins. As with Paul in Romans 7, we are doing the things we do not want to do and not doing the things we do want to do. After identification, it is the Lord Jesus living his life through the individual—a totally different quality of life.

The transformation may be gradual or sudden; but it is real in either case. Occasionally, there is a period of near euphoria because of the peace and freedom that is realized. This may last for hours or days. But, inevitably, self sneaks back into control as represented by the dip after the peak has been reached. Since the person is down, with self back in control, he is a prime target for Satanic attack. Satan always hits us while we are down! In fact, this is the only time he can really get to us. The first attack is usually hard on the heels of the identification realization. Being forewarned, we should be forearmed. The Word tells us that we should not be ignorant of Satan's devices (2 Corinthians 2:11). Also, "Resist the devil and he will flee from you" (James 4:7).

When we revert to self-control, the remedy is the same as when victory was realized in the first place—to reckon or account ourselves to be dead to sin (Romans 6:11). It is not a one-time experience which insures constant victory, but it must be a "daily" or "alway" reckoning upon our deliverance to the cross. Jesus declared, Luke 9:23: "If any man will come after me, let him deny *himself* and take up his cross *daily* and follow me." Paul expressed the same idea in 2 Corinthians 4:11: "For we which live are *alway* delivered unto death for Jesus' sake that the life also of Jesus might be made manifest in our mortal flesh." The cross spells death and deliverance as far as the reign of flesh is concerned. We triumph always and only in Christ.

After a new sense of freedom is experienced as a result of entering into identification, it is necessary that we have *assurance* of identification. This is parallel to and just as vital as being sure of salvation. Unless we have assurance of salvation, we will not possess our possessions in Christ; unless we have assurance of identification we cannot rest in the finished work of Christ. This is particularly important when we revert to self for the first time. Based on feelings, our inclination may be to conclude "*I* lost it. *I* won't ever have that joy again. *I* didn't read enough. *I* didn't pray enough." *I, I,I*–self in control and indulging in self-pity.

If we are certain that identification is a reality, we can be assured that we will never lose our stage of growth. We can no more go back across Jordan (as will be explained in chapter 4), than we can go back across the Red Sea. After identification, however, the battles are more severe than before, *if* we try to fight them in our own strength. If we do not have assurance based on his Word and corroborated in our experience, we're very likely to think it wasn't real and that we were kidding ourselves all the while. Just as we acknowledged our sins and were forgiven after salvation, we are now to acknowledge self and "alway" be "delivered unto death for Jesus' sake" that we might be restored to victory.

The only place of triumph is in Christ, not in self: "Now thanks be unto God which always causeth us to triumph *in Christ* and maketh manifest the savor of his knowledge by us in every place" (2 Corinthians 2:14).

So long as the Lord Jesus is in control we will be up; when *we* are in control, we will be down. In the beginning, there may be a transferring of control back and forth from self to Christ until we learn how to exercise our wills that he might more consistently live his life through us. This is a lifetime learning experience, but we gradually find it more supernaturally natural to permit him to retain control. Philippians 1:6 promises, "Being confident of this very thing, that he which hath begun a good work in you will perform it until the day of Jesus Christ."

Identification with Christ does not constitute maturity; it signifies, rather, our becoming spiritually adult. It is very similar to age twenty-one physically at which we become legally adult, but there is much maturing that must take place afterward. The ups and downs are some of the growing pains of maturing spiritually.

Referring back to the curve showing the physical decline, we can now indicate some correlations. If we are maturing spiritually as we should, the physical decline is not fraught with nearly as many dangers from an emotional standpoint. As we lose physical strength we can draw from the Lord according to our need. As we continue to draw from him, we can maintain our emotional stability while increasing in wisdom and favor with God and man. Conversely, when we are spiritual dwarfs and are continually harassed with the exigencies of life, our aging bodies are inadequate to cope with the emotional demands. This sets the stage for a neurotic break or a variety of escape mechanisms.

It should be pointed out again that there is no reason why it should be many years after salvation that we enter into spiritual adulthood. This is our birthright, and it can be possessed immediately upon experiencing salvation.

The ups and downs after identification are usually more violent in new Christians due to lack of grounding in the basic principles of the Christian life. However, these new believers usually stabilize in a short period of time.

Which of the lines most nearly represents your life? Only as you are willing to be guided in an objective assessment or spiritual inventory by the Holy Spirit can you mature into a deeper and more wonderful relationship with our precious Lord. Don't stand still; go on! Abandon all rights to the helm of your life and claim all that he is for all that you need, and he will make you what he intended you to be.

WHEN LIFE IS LIKE A WILDERNESS

The previous chapter presents a method of graphically depicting spiritual growth which has proven exceedingly valuable in helping troubled Christians assess their spiritual condition or state. However, it was developed by man and must be accepted as such. In this chapter a similar purpose is intended, but a scriptural analogy is used for which there is more than sufficient warrant.

The journey of the children of Israel from Egypt into Canaan is a comparison for the stages of spiritual growth in the Christian. The Old Testament book of Joshua furnishes some of the most valuable illustrations of defeat and victory; and the New Testament book of Hebrews offers striking comparisons. Hebrews 4:11 refers to their "example of unbelief." The results of both belief and unbelief are carefully detailed.

God deals with us as individuals in similar manner to the way he dealt with the children of Israel as a nation. As you see in the diagram, their progress was from Egypt to the Wilderness to Canaan. God promised the land of Canaan to the children of Israel while they were yet in Egypt, just as he promises us a victorious life (Canaan) when we accept his Son, the Lord Jesus Christ. Egypt was a place of slavery for the children of Israel for 400 years, and it represents the slavery of sin into which each of us was born. The Red Sea was the means of deliverance for the children of Israel from

Pharaoh's army. When God opened the sea, they escaped across on dry ground. In the analogy, the Red Sea is typical of our deliverance from sin and bondage through trusting the Lord Jesus Christ. The Wilderness was a place of wandering for forty years where all the Hebrew adults who came out of Egypt except two died in the Wilderness—including Moses, their leader. Joshua and Caleb were the two believing ones who took God at his Word and went on into Canaan. Similarly, relatively few Christians enter the place of victory typified by Canaan.

The Red Sea is a picture of salvation; the Jordan River is a picture of identification with the Lord Jesus Christ. The children of Israel did not enter in because of unbelief (Hebrews 3:19), and most Christians follow their example. They feel that God ran fresh out of miracles the day they were saved! It certainly took a miracle to open the Red Sea, and it takes a miracle of grace to change the human heart at salvation. It also took a miracle to open the Jordan River, and it is a miracle of revelation when we see that we are crucified with Christ and are set free from our "wilderness wanderings" to enjoy freedom and victory in the Lord—the victorious life. As we shall see shortly, Canaan or the victorious life is not a flowery bed of ease, but the battles are the Lord's, *if* we let him fight them.

Now we have the setting before us. We can begin to evaluate our spiritual growth in light of this journey. It makes us much less apprehensive about the trip when we know the destination and are instructed about the pitfalls along the way. True, we must still cover the terrain; but we can chart a course which is attended by the least difficulty *if* we believe our map.

EGYPT (THE WORLD)	RED SEA	THE WILDERNESS (WANDERING)	JORDAN RIVER	CANAAN (THE LAND)
1. Self in Egypt	S	1. Egypt in self	I	1. Self dispossessed
2. Bondage to Satan	A	2. Bondage to self	D	2. Bondage to Christ
3. Sin	L	3. Carnality, immaturity, unbelief	E	3. Adulthood
4. Conviction of Holy Spirit	V	4. Discipline of Holy Spirit	N	4. Control by Holy Spirit
5. Christ as Judge	A	5. Christ as Savior and Lord	T	5. Christ as life
6. Control by Satan	T	6. Co-existence with Satan	I	6. Overt assault by Satan
	I		F	
	O		I	
	N		C	
			A	
			T	
			I	
			O	
			N	

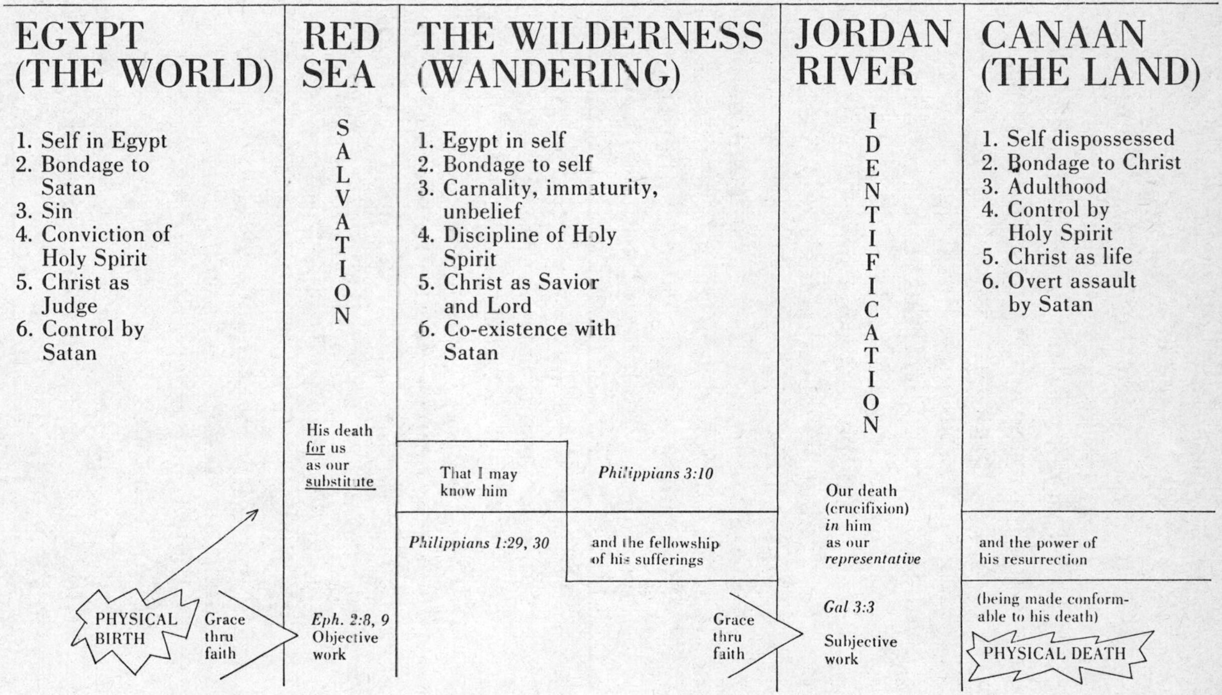

His death for us as our substitute

That I may know him — and the fellowship of his sufferings

Philippians 3:10

Our death (crucifixion) in him as our representative

and the power of his resurrection

Eph. 2:8, 9 Objective work

Philippians 1:29, 30

Gal. 3:3 Subjective work

(being made conformable to his death)

PHYSICAL BIRTH — Grace thru faith

Grace thru faith

PHYSICAL DEATH

DIAGRAM 13

In a journey across dangerous territory a map is indispensable if we are to reach our destination. When the author presented this diagram in a class once, a man was overheard to say, "I wonder if I am closer to the Red Sea or to the Jordan." When this man saw a map of his spiritual journey he was able to begin assessing his life. Not having realized that the Jordan was ahead, he probably thought that Canaan or the victorious life was Heaven. As a result, he was unaware of the necessary preparation for crossing the Jordan or experiencing the cross.

Most Christians are very bitter when this preparation by adverse circumstances begins, because they are ignorant of the purpose. Their only recourse is to fight God rather than to cooperate with him and patiently endure "the fellowship of his sufferings" (Philippians 3:10).

On a perilous journey we can be grateful for a map, but it is infinitely more comforting to have a guide with us who has made the trip before. Much of the apprehension is eased when the guide can prepare us in advance for the next segment of the journey and point out items of interest along the way. This is the purpose of the counselor in Spirituotherapy—to act as a spiritual guide. In this manner, the most direct routes can be taken and the stops and detours along the way can be explained.

Many times a person's suffering is not relieved immediately, but he can accept it more patiently when he understands the reason for it. Also, if he knows that immediately beyond that obstacle or trying circumstance is not only relief but deliverance, it is almost joy to endure the pain. Now let's begin tracing the spiritual journey from Egypt to Canaan. Beginning at the left of the chart and proceeding to the right with each item, let's look at the progression as we consider various aspects of the Christian life.

First, when we are born, our entire being is in Egypt; this is the starting point for each of us. Then, when we are saved or cross the Red Sea, we find that some of Egypt is still in us. The children of Israel looked back across the Red Sea and remembered the leeks and garlic they had there and gave Moses a bad time because they had only manna to eat. And we continue in some of the same thoughts and behavior so typical of us before we trusted Christ. This is due to the fact that self is very much in the ascendancy. Once we cross the Jordan or experience the cross, self is dispossessed. Although the ground gained must be maintained by continuous reckoning, the stage of growth is never lost.

Second, the time in Egypt is a period of being in bondage to Satan with him as our father and us as his slaves. After we have been Christians for some time, possibly many years, we begin to realize that we are in bondage to self. Paul described this vividly in Romans 7 where he admitted essentially, "The things I don't want to do, I am doing; the things I want to do, I am not doing." His internal turmoil brought him to the frustration he vents in Romans 7:24: "O wretched man that I am! Who shall deliver me from the body of this death?" He had seen self and its domination of his life for the horrible thing that it was. It made him so sick he couldn't stand himself. That's great! Each of us must be brought to that realization if we are to be willing to submit to the suffering of the cross.

Unless and until God turns on the searchlight of the Holy Spirit and illuminates his Word and our souls, we will not be "obedient unto death,

even the death of the cross" (Philippians 2:8).
Once we have been dealt with in this manner, we
are released from bondage to self and enjoy
being bound to Christ, which is real freedom.

Third, our life during the time in Egypt is
characterized by sin. We are born in sin and we
live in sin until its guilt has been dealt with by
the blood of Christ.

Most Christians spend all their lives in the
Wilderness, and some who eventually go on into
Canaan have spent the majority of their lives
wandering in the Wilderness. This is tragic but
true.

The time in the Wilderness is a time of
carnality, being controlled by self or the flesh.
Usage of the word *carnal* in evangelical circles
often connotes a Christian who is living in open
scandalous sin. This may be the case, but a
devoted minister who is working his heart out *for*
the Lord and has never experienced the cross
still has self in the ascendancy and is yet carnal.

We might also label this as a period of
immaturity—either spiritual infancy or spiritual
adolescence. Assuming that we yielded to
Christ as Savior *and* Lord at salvation, and we
have continued to remain in a yielded condition,
the length of time in the Wilderness is
determined by God. We should not apologize
for being a spiritual adolescent any more than
we should be ashamed of being a teen-ager. So
long as we are yielded to him, he takes us
through the stages of growth and maturity in a
time and manner commensurate with his
intended use of the completed vessel. We *can*
delay the process by an unyielded heart. It is the
Holy Spirit's move, if we stay yielded. Many
times during the process, it is necessary for us to
be subjected to adverse circumstances so that our

[96]

surrender is renewed, thus demonstrating God's sovereignty.

Finally, it can be a period of unbelief as it was with the Children of Israel. They knew God had opened the Red Sea, but they didn't think he could open the Jordan. Many Christians forget that salvation is a miracle and do not expect God to continue his work of grace in their hearts; therefore, they do not enter into the victorious or abundant life because of unbelief. Many do not even know that the Spirit-filled life is a live option for them. They seem to feel that it is only for a select few who are God's pets and that they are destined to live a life of defeat, failure, and frustration. Poor teaching of progressive sanctification can nurture this stalemate in spiritual growth.

This is the result of both ignorance and unbelief—sometimes fostered by the erroneous teaching that the Jordan is physical death and that Canaan is Heaven. So people are conditioned not to expect victory and peace here on Earth! They are taught that they must be saved and that they are going to Heaven when they die and that Christ may return at any moment. But in the meantime, it is just a *mean* time! The life of victory and power is for each of God's children; but resurrection power only follows crucifixion, and few seem willing to submit to its suffering. Even though our death in Christ is an accomplished fact at our new birth, the experiential realization of it usually comes through anxious times.

Fourth, the work of the Holy Spirit during the time in Egypt is conviction of sin. A thorough conviction of sin is essential before we will admit our need of the Savior. We must realize our sinfulness and lostness before we can be

[97]

saved. After we trust the Lord Jesus, the work of the Holy Spirit is to discipline or teach us. Scripture uses the word *chasten* in this regard. Hebrews 12:11 states, "Now no chastening for the present seemeth to be joyous, but grievous: nevertheless afterward it yieldeth the peaceable fruit of righteousness unto them which are exercised thereby." When the discipline of the Holy Spirit has accomplished its purpose, we experience release from control by self and enjoy control by the Holy Spirit. We can not be filled or controlled by the Holy Spirit until self and its hold are broken. And this is only accomplished by the cross.

Fifth, during our stay in Egypt, Christ is our judge. We are at enmity with God and remain so until we have been reconciled through the blood of the Lord Jesus Christ. Romans 5:8 states that "God commendeth his love toward us, in that, while we were yet sinners, Christ died for us." Once we receive him (John 1:12) we become sons and are no longer at enmity with him. During the Wilderness time he is our Savior; and when we yield totally to him, he also becomes our Lord. This is the most important decision a Christian ever makes.

This unreserved yielding to him is "our reasonable service" (Romans 12:1) and is prerequisite to our going beyond the Jordan and knowing the Lord Jesus as our very life. Paul said, "For to me to live is Christ ..." (Philippians 1:21). This must take place by revelation; we can understand it intellectually, but the life of Christ becomes real within us as he is revealed by the Holy Spirit. Paul testified that "it pleased God, who ... called me by his grace, to reveal his Son *in* me ..." (Galatians 1:15, 16). The Lord Jesus Christ is revealed *to* us at salvation, but he must be revealed *in* us. Second Corinthians 4:11 states: " ... we are alway delivered unto death for Jesus' sake that the life also of Jesus might be made manifest in our mortal flesh." Others cannot see him in our lives until first he has removed *us* out of the way.

Paul states it another way in Galatians 4:19: "My little children, I travail in birth again until Christ be *formed* in you." He cannot be formed in us until he has first dealt with the ugly self that resists conformity to Christ. Both the need and the answer must come by revelation of the Holy Spirit. He must increase and we must decrease; we decrease to nothing so he can be everything—our very life!

Sixth, we must consider the work of Satan during the three periods of time. The time in Egypt is a time of total control by Satan. We are his subjects since he is the ruler of this world, and we are shackled by the bonds of sin even though we do not recognize it until the Holy Spirit begins to draw us to Christ. During the Wilderness period we more or less co-exist with Satan. He doesn't bother us very much because we are hardly worth his notice. Self is doing an excellent job of keeping things in a mess so he just sits back and says, "Go to it, Self!"

The time in Canaan is an entirely different matter. Here we can expect direct Satanic assault in a myriad of ways: attacks on our thought life, hindrances in our work, discouragement, sleepless anxiety, demonic harassment—varied and frequent subtle manifestations of the evil one. He is not stronger than our Lord, and he is a defeated foe; but we must not "be ignorant of his devices" (2 Corinthians 2:11). To be ignorant is to court disaster, because he goes about "seeking whom he may devour" (1 Peter 5:8).

It might be well to take a look at the battles in the land so that we are not surprised nor dismayed by the strife to be found there. Once the children of Israel were in the Land, they still had to possess the Land and they found it inhabited by seven tribes. The first battle to be fought in the Land was the battle of Jericho. The siege of this walled city could have been a much greater battle than any that they endured in the Wilderness if they had fought it with their own resources and asked God for a little help along the way.

They did not approach it this way—they followed God's directions explicitly and the walls fell down as they made the final shout (Joshua 6:20). They were cautioned by God not to take any of the "accursed thing" but to utterly destroy everything. But there was an Achan who was unwilling to be obedient. He stole some valuables and hid them in his tent (Joshua 7:21). And the result? The next battle they fought was a different story—they were almost decimated! They scurried back to camp to determine the cause of the defeat. God showed them Achan's disobedience and commanded that he and all his possessions be destroyed. In other words, self must be brought back to the cross that Christ might again be in control.

The next time they went into battle, God gave the victory as he promised (Joshua 8:1) because he was in control. God, not self, causes us to triumph (2 Corinthians 2:14). Victory is always and only *his* work in and through us. Paul emphasizes that "we are more than conquerors *through him* that loved us" (Romans 8:37).

Looking at the lower portion of the Wilderness

section of the chart, there is the breakdown of Philippians 3:10 beginning with, "That I may know him." Of course, we come to know him at salvation and continue to learn about him as we live with him. The next portion of the verse has been deliberately taken out of the order in which it appears in the verse to fit in with the order of our experience. The "fellowship of his sufferings" is our lot as we experience his cross. Upon total commitment, the processing so vital to our being forced to the cross is begun. After the work of the cross in our lives we can experience "the power of his resurrection." Only as we are at the cross can his power be manifested—and we must daily be "made conformable to his death."

When he is in control, he can exercise his power to his glory. He will never share his glory with another (Isaiah 48:11). According to Ephesians 1:19, 20, all of the power that God used in raising Christ from the dead is available in us which makes it imperative that "the excellency of the power be of him and not of us" (2 Corinthians 4:7). God demonstrates his power as we yield to him so that we can't consume it or use it for the fulfillment of our own lusts. When we attempt to do this, he withdraws his power until we are again at the cross, and he can manifest himself to his glory.

Some other comparisons and contrasts which may be observed follow. At salvation— illustrated by the Red Sea—we realize his crucifixion *for* us and appropriate his blood shed for our sins. At identification—typified by the Jordan—we realize our crucifixion *in* him and appropriate the victory his cross provides. Salvation is more of an *objective* work—something that is done for us. Identification is more *subjective* in nature—something that is done in us. In salvation Christ is our Substitute; in identification he is our Representative.

We entered into salvation by grace through faith; we enter into identification in precisely the same manner. Our salvation in all its stages is grace at the beginning, grace at the end, and grace all the way through. We are not worthy to be saved from sin; neither are we worthy to be saved from self. But God in his infinite mercy deigns to have fellowship with us as redeemed sinners and to fill us with his life, love, and power in order that he may be glorified. Then, just as Joshua and Caleb spied out the Land and came back with the minority report, we also must share with those in the Wilderness that the Land of Canaan is indeed the Promised Land flowing with milk and honey. However, like the faithful two, we must be prepared for rebuff because few Christians are receptive to the command, "Be filled with the Spirit" (Ephesians 5:18)—especially when they learn that they must first be emptied at the cross.

It usually takes considerable time and study before we are sufficiently established in the new life to be able to share effectively with those who are yet in the Wilderness. It seems that it takes at least a year for a person to be well enough grounded to be able to share with another without offending him. It usually takes considerably longer than that to learn to lead a person to the Jordan and go through the suffering with him as he proceeds downward to the cross. The person himself must take that step of faith into the Jordan before the water parts: "For we which have believed do enter into rest …" (Hebrews 4:3). "There remaineth therefore a rest to the people of God. For he that is entered into his rest, *he also hath ceased from his own works*" (Hebrews 4:9, 10). "Come unto me, all ye that labor and are heavy laden, and I will give you rest" (Matthew 11:28). Persons who are prepared by the Holy Spirit and have a clear view of the despicability of the flesh, or self-life, and an equally clear view of its scriptural destiny, the cross, are now ready to pray the "selfer's" prayer. An unsaved person controlled by sin is a sinner; a Christian controlled by self (the flesh) is a selfer (to coin a new term).

The unsaved person must concur with the scriptural conclusion that he is lost in sin and that Christ died for that sin and rose again. The carnal Christian must agree that there is nothing worthwhile in the flesh and the scriptural remedy is that he died with Christ and rose again victorious over the world, the flesh, and the devil.

The sinner trusts Christ as *Savior;* the "selfer" trusts Christ as *Life.* We are reconciled to God by the death of his Son but we are saved (from ourselves) by his life (Romans 5:10).

GOD'S PROCESSING TUNNEL

Egypt
As we embark on the journey of life
And partake in its burdens and cares;
Ere long we loathe the turmoil and strife,
And seek respite from its snares.

In vain we search for joy that endures
Among the pleasures and trinkets of Earth;
Only to find that which beckons and lures
Is empty and void of true worth.

On and on 'til the restless heart cries
For the relentless ache to cease;
Oh, for Someone to wipe tears from our eyes
  (Rev. 7:17)
  And flood our beings with peace. (Jn. 16:33)

At length we see that he who died
  Was acquainted with sorrow and grief;
  (Isa. 53:3, 4)
And we come confessing our sin and pride:
  (Rom. 10:9, 10, 13)
  And, in coming, experience relief. (Jn. 5:24; 8:32)

Wilderness
In this new-found Friend all grace resides
That abounds to our every need; (2 Cor. 9:8)
The promise is to him who in Jesus abides, (Jn. 15:5-7)
To him who from Self has been freed.

But the monster Self is a dauntless foe
That insists on ruling the life; (Rom. 7:18, 19)
So instead of the peace we fain would know
We encounter a new kind of strife.

As the battle rages and clouds are dark
And our way with heartaches is lined; (Rom. 7:24)
We almost give up; we almost give out—when hark;
  A promise: "... I will bring the blind ..."
    (Isa. 42:16)

Many are the doubts as he leads us along
By a path that we would not choose;
But, clinging to him, we can't go wrong,
Since our life to save we must lose. (Luke 9:23, 24)

As in a tunnel whose center is black
We yearn for light on our path;
In the wall of despair we search for a crack
That we might walk by sight—not faith. (2 Cor. 5:7)

The Spirit's discipline, reaching far and wide,
Denies the comfort we keep demanding;
But, as we take our place in the Crucified,(Gal. 2:20)
We find peace past all understanding. (Phil. 4:7)

Canaan
Now, as before, a new battle begins
For which we are ill-prepared
As Satan his fiery darts expends (Eph. 6:16)
To tempt us again to despair.

When he launches forth his savage attack (1 Pet. 5:8, 9)
To regain the ground he has lost,
We're tempted to quit and turn our back
On the warfare and its ultimate cost. (Eph. 6:12)

In the battle fierce with strength bereft,
We realize that all is but loss,
And retrace our steps to the place we left (2 Cor. 2:14)
As he delivers us alway to the cross. (2 Cor. 4:11)

As our mortal flesh shows our union with him,
Jesus' life will be made manifest;
And the things of this world will ever grow dim,
As we enter into rest. (Heb. 4:3)

* * * * * * *

Though your way seems hopeless and full of fears,
God is handling you in love, dear friend;
No matter how dark your tunnel appears,
Take heart, there is light at the other end.

C. R. SOLOMON

[105]

INTELLECTUAL UNDERSTANDING— THEN WHAT?

You may be thinking that this all makes sense intellectually and theologically, but how does it become a reality in *my* life? No, this is not just more knowledge to add to your collection of useless facts. This is the life that God wants for *all* of his children, and he has no favorites!

So often we think that this all sounds well and good for choice saints like the Apostle Paul, D. L. Moody, Hudson Taylor, and those special few. But it is for us! While it is not attainable, it is obtainable. When we experience the Lord Jesus Christ as our life we haven't "arrived"— unless it is at the bottom! The cross was a place of humiliation, suffering, shame, and loneliness for our Lord. It will be the same for us—we are certainly not better than he!

You may be also prone to feel that this sounds plausible for others, but that you are too far gone or too worthless or too something else for God to do such a miracle in your life. Well, here is good news for you; it is just such persons that God meets and sets free.

One lady came for counseling who had been diagnosed paranoid schizophrenic and had spent time at a nationally known clinic and seven years in private psychiatric treatment. When she was told point blank that God would completely deliver her from all of these symptoms, she looked the counselor straight in the eye and exclaimed her total disbelief that such a thing was possible. Less than four months and ten interviews later, God met her in a crisis experience and removed the symptoms!

Each tormented soul who comes feels, "It just can't possibly happen in *my* life." But God is faithful to his Word and his calling. He meets us who are willing to meet him. His promise is that he will draw near to us if we draw near to him (James 4:8); he *doesn't* promise to chase us down!

Some come for counseling who want their lives to continue pretty much *status quo*, but without the problems they present. They are not willing to submit to a *total* transformation. To be honest with them, the counselor must tell them to go out and suffer some more. As long as they are trying to bargain with God they may as well forget it. When they are willing to drop their conditions and meet his, then they are candidates for deliverance and will probably continue in counseling until they are set free.

If we sincerely desire deliverance, we must be willing to commit ourselves first to the Lord and then to a concentrated study program. This is an integral part of the counseling process as well. Since it is our meeting with God that is going to be our source of deliverance, we must spend time in his Word and in studying books about spiritual growth.

After the intellectual understanding of the way of deliverance then we must continue to study the Word to comprehend more clearly our position in Christ. As we do, and reckon or account it to be so, the Holy Spirit will make it real in our experience. As has been stated earlier, it may be gradual or it may be a crisis. Very possibly it will be even more real and transforming than the day we trusted Christ. Ours is to study and look to him; his is to reveal the life of the Lord Jesus in us.

As we begin to reckon upon these truths and God begins to deal with us, the ensuing struggle takes many forms. Some of the problems which are regularly experienced by those in the counseling process are described in the remainder of this chapter.

1. After Total Commitment

Persons are frequently led by sincere and well-meaning Christian counselors or pastors to believe that the Lordship of Christ or total commitment is the epitome of the Christian experience. Let's enlarge a little on the idea of total commitment.

When a believer comes to GFI for counseling he is shown that any further progress in his spiritual maturity and subsequent deliverance from enslaving emotional symptoms is contingent upon his *total* surrender. The emphasis is put on the *total*, and it is not made easy because it *is not* easy! It means surrender with no reservations—not friends, family, profession, future, possessions. Anything that we are or have or might be is included in such a complete surrender. If we are dead serious, we are going to be seriously dead! Our surrender is basically our permission for our Father to take us to the cross.

Consider the story of the hen and the hog who were discussing the poverty program and what possible part they might have in the alleviation of hunger and suffering. Each made several suggestions which were refused by the other. Finally the hen came up with what she considered to be a sterling idea: they could provide some hungry unfortunates with ham and eggs! The hog considered this briefly and replied, "You would! For you, that is a *contribution*; for me, it is *total commitment*."

[109]

It is well to remember that *such a commitment is an act of our will; our emotions may cry out against it,* but our mind knows on the basis of God's Word that there is no other way. So, by a definite act of the will we choose God's way for our life, not having any advance knowledge as to what this may entail. But, knowing that his way is the best way, whatever it is, we yield to him and trust him to bring it about in our lives (Psalm 37:5).

It is necessary to point out that this surrender and identification are not always simultaneous. In cases where a Christian is at his wit's end and learns of his position in Christ and yields to God completely, the Holy Spirit reveals it to him, and it becomes real in his experience at once. This is the exception rather than the rule, however, in the average Christian's experience. The experienced counselor may see a large percentage of clients surrender and appropriate Christ as life simultaneously, since he is dealing with a biased sample—those who are in dire need.

Generally, the condition of the counselee actually worsens after the inception of counseling and subsequent surrender. This is only logical because God first has to take him through a reduction process where he is reduced to nothing so that Christ might be everything—his all in all! But again, if a person knows *why* he is getting worse he does not push the panic button. He realizes the progress to the cross is downward. Only when we understand the purpose of the suffering can we appreciate the "fellowship of his sufferings" (Philippians 3:10).

Many times total commitment takes place at salvation, which should always be the case, or shortly afterward. Then a person may go through many years of preparation for the cross. If he is totally yielded, the length of time it takes for him to experience the cross is determined by the sovereignty of God. We can delay his work in our lives by hardening ourselves against his chastening (Hebrews 12:11).

We have seen several persons who were saved and who understood their identification with Christ at the same time. This resulted in a depth work by the Holy Spirit making the Christ-life instead of the self-life evident from the beginning. This is not to say that they were immediately mature as was explained in Chapter 3.

One such person was a young man who had recently spent four months in a mental institution. He was taking a bottle of tranquilizers in a week's time and barely coping with life. He declared himself to be an agnostic, but said he was willing to consider God's answer to his needs. In the first interview he yielded to the claims of Christ and was admonished to refrain from trying to live a Christian life. Returning the following day he expressed ideas about how *he* should live the new life. This was exactly what he was instructed *not* to do. He was again shown that it must be the life of Christ lived out in him.

That night, he was planning to attend a ball game. Usually a handful of tranquilizers was needed to enable him to remain in a crowd, due to his paranoia. On this night, however, he had left his apartment and forgotten his tranquilizers! Inasmuch as he had not been without them since he left the institution, he started back to get them when he thought, "The Lord doesn't need any tranquilizers!"

With that calming assurance he went to the game—tranquilized only by God's Spirit—and enjoyed the best time he had experienced in twenty years.

Assuming that we remain yielded to God's processing and shaping, the length of time depends upon his projected usage of our lives to his glory. We cannot share with those who suffer if we ourselves have never suffered (2 Corinthians 1:3, 4). Our suffering is a time of learning and training for future usefulness. It can be an occasion for drawing closer to the Lord as he shapes his vessel like a potter molding his clay. Too often, we are prone to question whether the stages of shaping are necessary as the Master Potter unerringly molds us more perfectly into the image of his Son.

Another very significant point to keep in mind relative to surrender is that even though it is total in scope, it must be carried out in practice, item by item. In other words, we have surrendered the whole package, but he must now deal with everything in the package. Therefore, we find that many times afterward, we are holding on to this or that; but he gently breaks our grip—unless we are stubborn. Then he must take stronger measures.

But he that called is faithful! (1 Thessalonians 5:24). It is almost as if we are being literally carried to the cross and we grasp for everything we pass on the way! In his sovereign love, he remembers our initial surrender and continues to bring his way to pass in our lives (Psalm 37:5). What comfort there is in this knowledge! Even though we resist him and think we have reneged on our commitment and missed his will for our lives, he is faithful to perform that which *he* has begun (Philippians 1:6).

[112]

2. Morbid Introspection

A great percentage of Christians, and neurotics almost without exception, spend much time in looking inward. This may be searching for sin or evaluating this or that behavior or trying to justify their own existence. Those who feel exceedingly inferior and worthless may spend the majority of their time contemplating their hopeless plight. The result? The more they look inward the more miserable they become—in spite of the fact that they may view their self-searching and self-condemnation as proof of their sincerity, or as a kind of punishment by which they get even with themselves! They may even conclude that God surely will reward them for their futile attempts to probe and purge and somehow make themselves acceptable in his sight.

This searching process is not only interminable and depressing to the believer, it is repugnant to God. Psalm 139:23, 24 highlights the fact that it is God's job to do the searching: "[You] Search me, O God, and [You] know my heart; [You] try me, and [You] know my thoughts; And [You] see if there be any wicked way in me, and [You] lead me in the way everlasting." But all too many Christians by their action (or inaction) read the verses: "[I] search me, O God, and [I] know my heart; [I] try me and [I] know my thoughts; And [I] see if there be any wicked way in me, and [I] lead me in the way everlasting." That's Psalm 139:23, 24— according to most Christian neurotics!

At best, our searching can only turn up garbage; and sorting garbage is a most depressing avocation. Too, if we could ever complete the interminable task, we would wind up with neatly sorted piles of garbage, but still overlook the source of all the garbage—self. When God turns on the searchlight, he is much more interested in dealing with the source than with the results. And he is always ready to "forgive our sins and to cleanse us from all unrighteousness" (1 John 1:9). But it must grieve him to see us plagued by the same besetting sins year after year. He always abhors sin and desires to rid us of it by putting it under the *blood of Christ*. Self— the flesh—is also the object of his abhorrence, and he yearns to rid us of its control and dominion through the *cross of Christ*.

When an overly introspective person ceases or attempts to cease this useless and harmful indulgence of self, he usually feels guilty for falling down on God's job! He always fails at it because he is playing God. That's a sure-fire way to fail.

LOOKING TO JESUS
(Psalm 139:23, 24)
Looking to Jesus (Heb. 12:2)
  And not at my sin,
I am prevented
  From looking within.

His is to search me
  And know all my heart;
The things there he finds
  To me doth impart.

His is to try me
  And know all my thoughts;
His mind become mine (Phil. 2:5)
  To cover my faults.

His to "see if there be
  Any wicked way in me,"
To purge me from self, (Gal. 2:20)
  In him I am free. (Jn. 8:32).

His is to lead me
  In th' e'erlasting way,
That over my being
  He holds complete sway.

Now I can give in
  To his slightest nod;
I've taken my place
  And quit playing God.

Looking to Jesus
  While he looks within,
I look not at self;
  And he keeps from sin.

C. R. SOLOMON

3. Spiritual Vertigo

This is a malady which affects a great majority
of Christians. The name is derived from a
condition pilots sometimes encounter in which
their senses tell them that their aircraft is in a
totally different attitude from that indicated by
their instruments. They have been accustomed
to flying by sight and by feel (a seat-of-the-pants
approach) so instrument flying presents a new
challenge—they must fly by faith rather than by
sight. They must have complete confidence in
their instruments to the point that their faith will
override their feelings.

Sometimes, a pilot's feelings tell him that his
plane is level when he is really flying with one
wing down on take-off or landing. If his right
wing is tipped and he goes into a right bank, he
spins towards the ground. Or he may be cruising
along and suddenly is overwhelmed with the
feeling that he is upside down. Everything in
him cries out that he must turn the plane over!
Now, he looks at his instruments and is
confronted with the fact that he is right side up

and everything is normal. Which is he to believe? His feelings or his instruments? Of course, he must believe his instruments; he must act on the facts which are more reliable than his feelings.

As Christians we are consistently faced with the same dilemma. If we are well adjusted psychologically, there is not as much disparity between our feelings and the facts. However, a person who *feels* inferior, insecure, inadequate and unacceptable is continuously faced with a set of emotions which are at variance with the facts or reality. Therefore, he must distort the facts to agree with his feelings or employ some defense mechanism to permit him to cope with an untenable situation. Neurosis is said to be the distortion of reality. A person may *feel* inferior when he really isn't; in fact, most who have extreme inferiority feelings excel in many areas. But because they *feel* inferior, there are many things they will not attempt, or they withdraw from certain situations—not because they cannot perform but because they *feel* they cannot. Naturally, this causes much frustration and internal conflict, and it is compounded because with their mind they *know* they can perform, but their emotions cry out, "No!"

It goes without saying that we cannot change our emotions, but *in Christ* we are not called upon to change our emotions. This, too, is God's job; and, if we try to do it, it is just so much more self-effort which is bound to come to naught. When we experience the Lord Jesus Christ as our life, he changes our emotions. All of these changes do not occur instantaneously. The transformation is effected as we begin to place all of our confidence in our Instruments—the infallible Word of God. With our mind we must

[116]

realize that God's promises are true and then determine with our will to act upon them. Even if we *feel* that they are untrue or *feel* that God will not perform these promises for us, he will still honor his word and keep his promises to us (2 Timothy 2:13). As we consistently *will* to deny our feelings and *will* to place our confidence in our infallible Instruments, our feelings will increasingly come into line with the facts. When this happens we are no longer neurotic and our feelings are consistent with our faith in the facts!

4. Spiritual Surgery

Colossians 2:11 reveals that in Christ we are circumcised with the circumcision made without hands in putting off the *body of the sins of the flesh* (the flesh or self-life). Paul cries out, "O wretched man that I am! Who shall deliver me from *the body of this death*" (Romans 7:24). Then he goes on to discover that his victory is "through Jesus Christ our Lord."

Here we find the identification truths, the experiential removal of self as the master of the life—much like physical surgery. The analogy has many similarities.

Before physical surgery there is generally, though not always, a period of time during which a person suffers from certain symptoms. This suffering convinces him that he has a need. These symptoms may plague one in various forms for several years before a person sees a physician or before the surgery actually takes place. When the adverse effects on the life are severe enough and the pain is no longer endurable, he realizes that something must be done. Usually he will try several remedies to suppress the symptoms in a vain effort to avoid surgery.

Christians also try everything from hedonistic pursuits to compulsive Christian service. Or they may hit the tranquilizers. Or seek spiritual "experiences" of all kinds. Anything is tried in order to avoid the spiritual surgery which must take place if they are to be set free and to be unhindered in their service for the Lord. It is similar to patients who try all of the remedies and escapes until surgery becomes unavoidable. Even after it is known that surgery is the only way out, most persons postpone it as long as possible though the pain seems unendurable.

Once the diagnosis is made, it gives some relief if the patient knows that it is not terminal. There will be pain involved, but his life again will be a pleasure after the surgery is healed. Understanding the suffering removes the mystery even though the pain persists. The problem can now be dealt with realistically. Now we understand that whatever the adverse circumstances we are experiencing, it is permitted of God to point up the necessity of spiritual surgery.

God does not allow this for punishment but for discipline or chastening so that our lives may be more free and joyful than ever before.

Once all of the escapes are blocked off, we must endure the surgery. As preparations are made for the operation, the patient must be rendered helpless. You can imagine how ludicrous it would be for the patient to jump around on the table in an attempt to "help" the surgeon. If the patient stirs, more anesthesia is administered. The surgeon neither wants nor needs the patient's help.

In similar manner, as God prepares us for spiritual surgery, he must take us through the process of defeat, failure, and suffering to render us helpless. Otherwise, he would find us moving around on the table trying to "help" him. Usually, we have done so much to "help" him up to this time that we involuntarily, if not by intent, try to help in the process of surgery where self is rendered inoperative (Romans 6:11). The surgeon of the body uses the scalpel; the Surgeon of the soul applies the cross to the source of the problem—self.

The divine Surgeon's purpose is not merely to take away the pain and restore us to our former way of life where self has dominated but to enable us to enjoy the reign of the Christ life instead of the self-life. Sometimes the surgery is short, and sometimes it is lengthy depending on the nature of the case. In other words, the spiritual surgery may take place gradually or it may be a crisis experience; in either event the result is the same—a transformation (Romans 12:2) or renewing of the mind.

Then there is always the convalescence after surgery. This is rarely a smooth, uphill process. There are normally many ups and downs as we adjust to the new life. We may frequently revert to the old life with its defeats and frustrations— only to require a return to the surgery of the cross (Luke 9:23; 2 Corinthians 4:11).

Finally, as in physical surgery, we delight to tell others of our successful surgery; and we are more than delighted to recommend the eminent and *only* Surgeon so that our friends, too, may know the joy and rest in the new life—the Christ life!

5. *Suffering in Perspective*

Meaningless suffering is agony in the extreme. The physical pain may not in itself be unbearable, but the mental anguish becomes a cruel

[119]

taskmaster. When misunderstood, suffering causes despair, defeat, and frustration. And often its concomitants are resentment, bitterness, hostility, and depression. If, however, we can apply God's lenses to our eyes and see the general end he has in view, then the suffering affords an entirely new perspective. We may have endured untold suffering for years; but when we come to appreciate it as the "fellowship of *his* sufferings," we recognize that suffering is indeed a privilege (Philippians 1:29).

One lady came for counseling who, like the woman in Mark 5:26, had "suffered many things of many physicians." She recited her tale of woe. After about fifteen years with psychologists and psychiatrists, Christian and secular, in addition to the rounds of ministers and counselors, she was almost nonfunctional. The counselor's comment on her condition was simply, "Wonderful!" Her look was one of amazement, not amusement. But as she was shown the necessity of coming to the end of self, she began to see that sympathy was the last thing she needed. Years of such treatment had merely served the purpose of driving her farther down.

God used this, though, to force her to the end of self. Realizing the reason for her suffering, she quit fighting God and trusted him to continue it until he had accomplished his purpose. She cooperated with him as he rapidly took her to the cross. In a very short time, she was released from the so-called "mental illness" for which she had endured years of symptomatic treatment.

6. *The Death Blow*

Suffering takes place over a period of time, as self is crucified by degrees. Yet there must come the time when self yields completely to the cross. There are many signs of the end's approach. Usually, there is a period of deep anxiety just prior to the end. As in physical death, sometimes there is sudden "death" without a struggle. In other cases there are the death throes as life leaves the body. Even though a patient may be dying of cancer, and actually yearns to die because of the excruciating pain, as he begins to die he instinctively tries to hold on to life. Similarly, even though a believer realizes that he is being drawn to the cross, it is almost as if the Lord has to drag him kicking and screaming as he reaches for everything he passes on the way.

If we have presented our bodies as "a living sacrifice" (Romans 12:1), he is not going to heed our pleas for comfort until the sacrifice is consummated. The Father had to refuse to ease the awful agony of his Son on the Cross as he cried out, "My God, my God, why hast thou forsaken me?" Just so he cannot—he *must* not—ease the burden until his gracious work is finished in our experience. The Lord Jesus had no respite from his suffering until he died. It was only after the suffering that Jesus entered the resurrection life.

In our lives the suffering of the crucifixion precedes the power of the resurrection. Second Timothy 2:11 assures, "If we suffer, we shall also reign with him." We cannot bypass the cross and still know its power or experience the cross without its suffering. Nor can the theology of the cross substitute for the experience of the cross in our lives. It is much more romantic to read about the trials and tribulations of great saints as God prepared them for ministry than it is to experience this ourselves.

Even though the atonement for sin was

[121]

vicarious in that Christ shed his blood for our sins and in so doing gave us his life, his cross must become the *experienced* cross before his victory and power can be ours. In other words, we must enter into his life before we can share his death. As the corn of wheat has to fall into the ground and die to produce fruit, so also must we enter into his death before his Life can be manifest in us in the bearing of much fruit (John 15:5). "Whosoever will save his life must lose it" (Luke 9:24a).

As we approach the cross we must be brought to the utter end of our own resources. In doing so there are times when we think we can not go on—that God doesn't love us or he wouldn't let us go through these difficult times. Or we may suspect that our unsaved or saved mate is bringing all of this on us, or that it is the result of our sin (and it may be). We may even conclude that God delights in punishing us— perhaps because we do not have enough faith. All of these thoughts and many others may surge through our minds as we near the end of self.

Many times we try to "rescue" ourselves from this because we dread the pain or the humiliation. One by one God eliminates the avenues that offer some temporary relief. When we fear that there is no way out but death we have arrived at the truth. There isn't! However, suicide isn't the answer because the problem is not confined to the body—it has invaded the soul. Suicidal feelings are not at all uncommon during this period of time since we feel that our faith is so weak that even God could not possibly do anything in our lives. In his grace, he made a way that we can get rid of ourselves and yet stay here—the cross!

We have been brainwashed to think that we

must have greater and greater faith if God is to accomplish anything in and through our lives. In practice, however, we find that our faith progressively becomes weaker and weaker. Occasionally the physical strength is also diminished to the place where a person is all but immobilized. This is sometimes necessary so that he can get us out of his way until he can complete the work.

One lady in this situation discovered that she could not get out of bed. Her husband notified the Fellowship that he would have to call in a psychiatrist. After additional conversation he agreed to bring her to the office. She limped into the counseling room and slumped into a chair. Only with great effort could she converse. When she was asked if she knew what was happening, she replied, "I think he is finishing the work." The counselor agreed. Then she said very slowly, "I'm just afraid I will get in his way as I have in the past, and he will not complete the work."

"You don't have to worry about that," she was assured. "He isn't even going to give you enough strength to get in his way." She thought about that for a moment and then replied with measured words, "That's the happiest sad thought I have ever had." The counselor then shared with her this verse out of *The Living Bible* (Tyndale House):

"Even when we are too weak to have any faith left, he remains faithful to us and will help us, for he cannot disown us who are part of himself, and he will always carry out his promises to us" (2 Timothy 2:13). She received no strength until a day or so later when he set her free. His strength was made perfect in her weakness (2 Corinthians 12:9).

[123]

7. *The New Life*

When the process of this crucifixion experience is consummated, the result is spiritual resurrection life. Though it may be a gradual or crisis revelation, the transformed life with its freedom is the proof that the Christ-life has become a reality. The manifestation of his life is different in each person. It usually takes several months to a year for a person to become reacquainted with himself and to have some idea of what to expect by way of reaction to various circumstances. Many have made the statement, "I just do not know myself anymore." The reaction is much the same on the part of family members. Some spouses almost experience a state of mild shock as a result of being conditioned by past experience to expect unchanged behavior.

Although the stage of growth is never lost, the victory or joy of it may be as self returns to the ascendancy in the life. It is most difficult not to return to past patterns of behavior and "try to live the Christian life." It is well to memorize and claim Galatians 2:20; then at the beginning of each day we can reckon ourselves again and consistently to be dead to sin, and trust the Lord Jesus Christ to express his life. The will must be engaged at all times; we *will* and he empowers (Philippians 1:6).

During the day it is well to remind ourselves several times, "It is not I, but Christ" and to expect that he will govern our plans and actions. We are *not* to become introspective and test every thought and action to see if Christ is responsible or self or Satan; we are merely to commit the day and our life to him and trust him to control us and each situation to his glory. Committing, trusting, reckoning—all are terms indicative of a functional will.

It is well to realize that if we regress to self in control, the defeats we suffer may be valuable learning experiences if we are determined to see them as such and not panic at our loss of victory and the hurt to self.

Many experience more "down" time than "up" during the early weeks of the deepened relationship as they gain discernment concerning the reassertion of self and the attacks of the adversary which are certain to come.

The excitement of life under Christ's control makes each day a new adventure when we are at rest and trust him who is our life to cause "all things to work together for good" (Romans 8:28).

DOES IT REALLY WORK?

One half-skeptical counselee commented, "The theory sounds good, but I'll reserve my opinion until I see if it really works." The proof of the foregoing method of counseling is the final outcome. Was the goal accomplished; was the person's life changed? The goal in Spirituotherapy is a transformed life, not merely positive changes in behavior and attitudes. The following cases are reviewed to prove that such transformations can and do occur. These are shared also to demonstrate God's power and glory.

Many of those testimonies on the following pages have also been shared publicly. Almost all who have received counseling are willing to state either publicly or privately their backgrounds, previous therapy, and the results of Spirituotherapy. They have come from all walks of life. The age range has been from 7 to 80, the educational and intelligence levels have ranged from emotionally or intellectually retarded to those with doctor's degrees.

Since the goals are entirely different from psychotherapy, direct comparison is difficult if not impossible. Judged on similar grounds to psychotherapy, the estimated success rate is 60-80 percent. Almost all have shown some improvement if they continued beyond the first interview.

The initial interview is exploratory. At this time the person learns that he will be pointed toward a complete life transformation. If he is unwilling to face this prospect, he must settle for psychotherapy elsewhere and attempt to learn to live with the problem. Anyone who decides against proceeding with counseling on such a basis is not written off as a failure; he just isn't desperate enough to let God deliver him. The counselor may fail but the Holy Spirit has no failures.

Also, there are those who experience considerable improvement, which would be considered success in psychotherapy, who are not willing to give up all and be transformed. In Spirituotherapy, we are not satisfied with great improvement, we want to see each person free from his problem by being freed from self.

With some, the improvement gives impetus to study; and the release takes place subsequent to the termination of counseling. Resolution of guilt problems can give much relief even though the self problem remains. A sufferer from severe psychological symptoms rarely gets any permanent relief until the Lord Jesus Christ becomes his life.

Susan was middle-aged and had been diagnosed as "reactive depressive." She had been under psychiatric treatment for two decades, with stays of varying lengths in three different institutions. After three or four interviews Susan was still not ready to abandon all and let God deliver her. Consequently, she was again hospitalized under court order for three months with outpatient treatment continuing for another nine months.

When she called GFI again she was nonfunctional to the point where she could not write her own name. She was consuming eight tranquilizers per day and three sleeping pills at night. Finally she was ready for deliverance.

[128]

Within thirty hours after the phone call, God met her and completely delivered her from every vestige of "mental illness"! From a rundown "skin-and-bones" condition she gained seventeen pounds within two months. Her borderline diabetic condition disappeared as did the tension in her eyes that had been so obvious for fifteen years. Since her transformation she has spent most of her spare time helping others.

Nineteen years of therapy of all sorts—psychotherapy, drug therapy and electro-shock therapy. Such was Marge's history. At the time she came for counseling her drug consumption was five to eight pills every three to four hours plus fifteen tranquilizers and sleeping pills in the span of two hours at night. Though only in her thirties she had been diagnosed "manic depressive" with six-month cycles. She had received a shock treatment each week of the depression for the last three years. Though more than 100 such treatments had already been administered, the psychiatrists were resigned to giving her this therapy once a week during the depression for the remainder of her life. Psychotherapy, she was told, admittedly would do her no good, but the psychiatrists could experiment with two more drugs. After five interviews at GFI in eight days, God met her on the ninth day and gave her victory over depression. Within approximately two months she had led another person into the same truth.

Bob Walden, D.D.S., a professional man in the Denver area, had run the gamut from accepting Christ at age nine to becoming an agnostic, then an atheist, and back to an agnostic. At the time he attended a meeting where the author was speaking, he had tried most of the humanistic existential philosophies only to discover that all were dead ends and that he, too, was at the end of his ego strength.

As he heard the material in Chapter 4 presented, the Holy Spirit convinced him of the truth and his search was ended. The transformation in his life and later in his wife's has been deep and dramatic. Although Dr. and Mrs. Walden were psychologically well adjusted individuals, the changes in their lives and in their family would require most of a book to delineate. One change is the removal of alcohol from this man's life. For years he had tried vainly to give up drinking. But the Holy Spirit completely removed the desire for the taste and effect of alcohol. He now finds the thought of alcoholic beverages repulsive. He still considers this a miracle.

Ted had been troubled with obsessive thoughts for eighteen years which had all but driven him and his wife insane. Five years before coming to GFI he had spent a month in a church-supported mental hospital. He had received electroshock therapy and psychotherapy and had continued in private therapy periodically over the five-year period. The psychiatrists had informed him and his wife that they would have to learn to live with the problem. He went through thirteen Spirituotherapy sessions before he finally got serious with God and started studying; three days later he was released from symptoms while on the job.

A minister whom we shall call Cal was troubled with extreme anxiety. In acute attacks his pulse would soar to 150. After more than two years of therapy, including electroshock and drugs, his pulse was consistently at ninety-five, accompanied by rapid breathing and loss of energy. The anxiety increased as is usually the case after counseling at the Fellowship began. After five or six counseling sessions, one night at about 11:30 his pulse and breathing suddenly dropped to normal. So free inside was his sensation that he thought his soul was leaving his body. He was certain he was dying. Panic-stricken, he awakened his wife and insisted that she take him to the hospital. Very calmly she asked, "What will you tell the doctor—that your pulse rate and breathing are normal? He will send you to a mental institution." Also conscious of a return of his energy, he stayed up and studied and praised the Lord until the early morning hours.

Kim was a high school dropout who had been given to extreme fantasy. Emotional reactions had induced her to attempt suicide. Also the victim of a traumatic experience, she had received psychotherapy. She was up and down for a year before she finally gave up *everything* to God and experienced victory.

Hal was a voyeur and pedophiliac. He was unsaved when he came for counseling. He trusted Christ in the first interview and was completely delivered prior to the fourth interview three weeks later. This was attested to by his wife of several years and his immediate family.

Another kind of sex deviate, Jake was a homosexual who had been a Christian for several years. Although he had known the identification truths intellectually, God revealed them to him experientially in the first interview. He was utterly shocked at the simplicity of God's working. He, too, had believed the absurdity that homosexuality was an organic deficiency

[131]

rather than a spiritual problem, as defined in Romans 1.

Kay had been diagnosed "paranoid schizophrenic" and had been treated at a well known clinic seven years prior to coming for counseling. Her case history disclosed that she had been subjected to psychotherapy, drug therapy, and electroshock therapy in three different institutions. After approximately ten interviews, God met her at her home one morning. She wept all day. At the end of the day she was free from the symptomatology that had characterized her life.

John had been saved two years and was wearing a neck brace when he came for the first interview. He had been diagnosed as having rheumatoid arthritis and had a slight injury to his left shoulder. The physicians said he would eventually lose the use of his head completely, and he was already unable to turn it. Also, he could not lift his left arm. He was taking six Darvon capsules, six Tylenol tablets, and six analgesic tablets every four hours around the clock.

During the third interview, both and his wife bowed their heads and yielded totally to the Lord Jesus Christ. When he returned for the fourth interview he wore no neck brace and was taking *no* pills. Two months later, when he visited his physician, still without the brace, the startled doctor exclaimed, "You *must* be in pain!" He had been unable to work for a year; now he is self-employed.

Tammy was a preteen who fitted the description of a sociopathic or psychopathic personality. She had been going to a child psychologist and getting worse with each visit. Though a brilliant child and very personable, her insecurity and inadequate conscience development were a source of constant irritation to her parents. Her progress was slower than a corresponding adult, but her behavior has radically changed.

Hobart's behavior had been characterized by extreme frustration and hostility which he habitually vented on his wife. Violence was common and every door in the house was literally loose on its hinges. His wife sued him for divorce and ejected him from the home. After three or four weeks he decided that counseling would not be as bad as the loneliness. His wife was a Christian but he was not. After a few counseling interviews he came to Christ in a deep conversion which resulted in their marriage being restored.

Henry was retired and had been making the rounds of physicians of various kinds for about two years, complaining of dizziness and depression. Although a Christian for fifteen years, it wasn't until his second interview that God revealed to him his position in Christ, and he was completely free.

As a successful Christian businessman Larry had held every office in an evangelical church. He was well adjusted psychologically, but his wife had a history of psychological symptoms. Over the years her problems had taken their toll until he was beaten down by them. When he came back for the second interview, tears streamed down his face as he told how his life had been changed by the Holy Spirit's revelation of the life *in Christ*.

Billie was a beautiful girl who had undergone two and one-half years of psychotherapy, some of it in two institutions. Her agitation was so intense she could not sit during the early interviews. During the third interview she accepted Christ and most of the agitation and depression left immediately. Many areas of her life changed as did her interpersonal relationships.

Married as a teenager, Marla had borne two children and then divorced. She had suffered two nervous breakdowns and had attempted suicide three times. It was from the third institution that she came directly to GFI where she trusted Christ in the first interview. Her life radically changed from this point and most of her fears left instantly.

Hilda was in her fifties and for many years had fought psychological problems which affected her marriage. Although a devoted Christian, she did not know how God could remove these debilitating symptoms. Her husband was very understanding as she had to be on medication constantly to prevent open conflict. One interview was sufficient for the Holy Spirit to reveal to her the liberating power of her position in Christ. Upon returning to her home in another city, she did not relate anything to her husband; the change in her attitudes and behavior made it unnecessary. A brother whom she hadn't seen in some time observed the transformation though he was in the home only twenty-four hours.

A Christian, out of fellowship with Christ for many years and an alcoholic. That was Molly. To fortify her own position, she continually found fault with her husband. After several interviews God moved in her life in a deep way, and she was restored to fellowship and delivered from alcoholism. They are now actively working together in business and in an evangelical church.

Mike was a transvestite. Understandably his

confused sex role was having a negative influence on his marriage. After two or three interviews, the Lord took away his desire to wear women's clothing. He began to study the Bible systematically, and many changes were brought about in his life.

Cindy was a middle-aged lady who loved the Lord and yet had been on the verge of a nervous breakdown for years. She was unable to be effective in life or in her church. After hearing the author deliver two lectures on the material contained in this book, God met her and delivered her. Her husband reported that her medical bills were down to zero and that she had witnessed more in two weeks than she had in her entire married life.

Because she had twice attempted suicide, Katie came for counseling. She had never been free of her family's influence on her life and was making life miserable for her husband. A few interviews sufficed to give her spiritual and psychological freedom. Subsequently, she established a responsible relationship with her family which, in turn, enhanced her marital relationship.

Jane and Jim were on the brink of divorce, and Jane would not participate in sexual relations. She was very outspoken and firm in her position. Humanly speaking, nothing could change her attitude. After four or five interviews, she had an experience with the Lord which miraculously changed her attitudes. Now she speaks of how "bullheaded" she was, and the marriage is better than ever, including the sexual relationship.

Eunice was another whose marriage was threatened because her attitudes toward sex were completely negative. Both she and her husband had rejected each other. After a few interviews she experienced identification with Christ and these attitudes greatly changed.

Eight months of group psychotherapy and some individual therapy had failed to give relief to Elaine, who was troubled with extreme depression and visual and auditory hallucinations. She and her husband came for the first interview together. After a brief period of getting acquainted, the T-JTA test results were interpreted to them and the material in Chapter 2 was explained. A week later Elaine came for an individual interview. During this interview God met her and released her from the symptoms. Subsequently, her interrelationships with her family changed, she lost thirteen pounds in one month, and she led her own husband (already a Christian) into identification with the Lord Jesus Christ.

The preceding are but a few of the miraculous transformations in lives. It *does* require a miracle in each life. These and the others who have experienced a similar deliverance have all had periods of regression which have varied in duration and intensity. Since the psychological symptoms are a function of self, it follows that when self is again permitted control, the previous symptoms will reassert themselves to a lesser degree. Self *never* changes; the only reason the person is different is that Christ is the center of the life. When self is at the cross, Christ is *in* control; when self is back in control, we're *out* of control.

Do those who experience deliverance hold up? Despite the expected regressions to self-centeredness, almost all of those delivered are experiencing greater psychological freedom than ever before.

Those who have had the most difficulty, as expected, are those who will not discipline their lives to study and who do not act upon those choices indicated by Scripture to be theirs in continuously appropriating by faith their resources in Christ. Study is of prime importance in being set free by the Holy Spirit, and it is of equal importance in the maintenance of that freedom.

Before the first interview, the Taylor-Johnson Temperament Analysis was administered to almost all of those who have been counseled. Additional testing after a prolonged period will permit some valid objective data which has statistical significance.

Many of those delivered have expressed their willingness to participate in a panel discussion where therapists who are interested could get first hand data concerning the clients' deliverance through Spirituotherapy and their candid opinions of this counseling as compared to their experiences in psychotherapy.

ALONE TOGETHER

We walked alone together,
My precious wife and I,
Nor learned to share our burdens,
But only how to sigh.

Our hearts being knit in love
Yearned for sweet communion;
But it seemed that such a joy
Could not grace our union.

The burdens that we carried
Seemed oft too much to bear,
But no matter how we tried
We could not the trials share.

The burdens served God's purpose (Ps. 119:71)
To drive us to our knees;
As we fellowshiped with Christ (Phil. 3:10)
He taught us by degrees. (Isa. 28:9, 10)

As his purpose for our lives (Rom. 8:29)
Began to come to pass, (Ps. 37:5)
We saw that inner conflict (Phil. 1:29, 30)
Had been our training class. (Heb. 12:11)

The comfort that he gave us
Was ours to keep in store;
Those who likewise walk alone (Ps. 142:4)
Find comfort at our door. (2 Cor. 1:3, 4)

We praise our precious Saviour
In him our life is found; (Phil. 1:21)
Though we are ever failing
In him doth grace abound. (2 Cor. 9:8)

The fears that came between us
Were like a mighty tower;
But Jesus made them tumble
By his transforming power. (Rom. 12:2)

And now we walk together
* In growing harmony;*
Our burdens become lighter
* When borne by me and thee. (Gal. 6:2)*

As we share from heart to heart
* Our love is fused with peace;*
As the years slip swiftly by
* Our joy but knows increase.*

C. R. SOLOMON

MEET
THE DIVINE
COUNSELOR

Spirituotherapy is *God's* work. And, as in all other
types of ministry, he does his work through
those whom he has uniquely prepared to be
used in such a manner. He calls the men but
promises that he will do the work. This is stated
succinctly in 1 Thessalonians 5:24: "Faithful is
he that calleth you, who also will do it."

In most instances God calls a man to his
service, and then the man spends a period of time
in preparation for the work to which he has been
called. In the case of the author, this order was
reversed—the preparation preceded the call.
That is, the life experience of which suffering was
the vital ingredient was necessary before the
ministry was a possibility. The divine
Counselor had to deal with the counselor in the
same manner that was to be used in the practice
of Spirituotherapy. Therefore, the author
received his most valuable training in the
USAF. The acronym does not have the usual
connotation; it is not the United States Air Force.
The letters stand for the University of Suffering
and Affliction Furnace (Isaiah 48:10). After
years of suffering from psychological conflict
and the additional burden of holding a responsible
position in industry which was not fulfilling, the
deliverance described in the preceding
chapters became a reality in October 1965.
Since it was direct revelation and totally
unexpected, there was no preparation for the
turmoil which followed as a result of regression
to self and overt Satanic assaults.

In 1967 the author was led to begin work on a master's degree while still employed in industry. God's call to the ministry was confirmed in November of that year (Isaiah 58:10, 11). The master's was completed in December 1969, and God led in leaving the position in industry January 1970. The ministry of GFI started full time in February 1970 simultaneously with beginning doctoral work. Since this approach to counseling has not been taught in Bible schools and seminaries, all of the diagrams and the approach were evolved in the study and sharing which was done prior to and during the early months of counseling. The doctoral work was a continuation of this study with this book written in lieu of a dissertation.

Early in the author's preparation for counseling, God demonstrated that what he would do *through* us he first must do *in* us. In his mercy, he had to reduce the author to nothing so that he who called might also *do* the work. How gracious he is to let us endure "the fellowship of his sufferings" that we might know "the power of his resurrection" (Philippians 3:10). God's work as Counselor in dealing with the counselor does not end with having initiated the work; the counselor must be " ... alway delivered unto death for Jesus' sake that the life also of Jesus might be made manifest in our mortal flesh" (2 Corinthians 4:11). This, and all other work that is truly God's, must be done in the power of the Holy Spirit; he must be the Therapist! When the human heart is to be changed, it is " ... Not by might, nor by power, but by my Spirit, saith the Lord of hosts" (Zechariah 4:6).

As has been stated previously, the counselor in Spirituotherapy serves as a spiritual guide, not a therapist. The counselor must be called of God to this specific ministry of leading souls into a depth relationship with Jesus Christ. It is not so much a technique to be learned as a relationship to be shared. A psychologist or psychiatrist may be a devoted Christian and yet not be used of the Lord in this manner. He may instruct a person about spiritual realities that he has not experienced, much as he would use textbook knowledge and therapeutic techniques. But he can only lead a person to spiritual depths that he himself has plumbed.

To do this will demand a willingness to forsake and repudiate the role of therapist and let the Holy Spirit make the necessary changes in the life of the counselee. This is one of the most difficult things to learn—or to unlearn. After having learned, and possibly used, the techniques of therapy it is almost second nature to apply them. Especially when the person who sits across the desk is extremely anxious and agitated, the counselor feels, "*I* must help him." To sit back and relax and let the Lord do the work is much more difficult. The counselor may feel that he is doing absolutely nothing for the person—and *he* really isn't! The prayer of the counselor must be that at all times he will be kept to the cross that the Holy Spirit may have free rein to work unhindered in and through him.

There is no attempt made to discern when the Holy Spirit is doing the work and when the counselor is. The counselor yields himself and trusts God for his anointing and leading as he proceeds with each individual.

The prime purpose of this book is to deal with intrapersonal (within the person) conflict. In the matter of spiritual growth, as in salvation, God deals with us as individuals. There may be

[143]

problems in relationships with others as in the marriage relationship, but there is no need to delve into the intricacies of personality psychodynamics, interactions, and behavior patterns. The basic problem is not with the relationship, but with the self-centered lives of those involved in the relationship.

For instance, each partner has a deep-seated notion as to what is expected of the other. This is why very few of the troublesome situations in a marriage are really "marriage" problems. Even problems of a sexual nature are rarely inherent in the marriage itself.

Most persons come for counseling because of a besetting problem which usually involves others. This problem serves as the impetus to force them to examine their own relationship to the Lord Jesus Christ. When a person experiences the Lord Jesus Christ as his *life* he begins to relate to others in an entirely different manner.

Since we are made up of body, soul, and spirit, it is necessary to understand as completely as possible the physical, psychological, and spiritual difficulties that a person may be experiencing. There have been several cases where a person has had extensive previous therapy and yet did not understand the genesis of his psychological symptoms. Although it is not absolutely necessary, it is comforting for a person to understand why he behaves as he does. In some cases a person has learned more about the nature of his psychological conflict in the first or second interview than he did in several interviews or several years in psychotherapy. A very common complaint is that "the psychiatrist never told me anything; he just let me do all the talking."

In summary, the counselor at GFI does not hesitate to discuss psychological symptoms for purposes of understanding; he *does* refuse to do therapy. No matter what the nature of the psychological symptom, which is functional as opposed to organic in nature, *appropriating our position in Christ will alleviate the conflict.* If an organic problem is present or suspected, the counselor works closely with the counselee's physician.

Usually, the first interview is sufficient to gain rapport with the individual and assure him that the counselor has a basic understanding of the problem presented and his emotional state. In fact, half of the first interview is enough in the vast majority of the cases. The counselor then has the opportunity to begin sharing the answer in somewhat the same manner presented in this book. Most of the sessions are about half counseling and half teaching. The order for the teaching varies under the leading of the Holy Spirit with each individual. The counselor is merely a tool in the hands of the Holy Spirit to be used as is appropriate in each unique situation.

You have read the preceding material in somewhat the role of the counselee. As in the counseling situation, there is nothing you can do to rid yourself of the turmoil or defeat which you may be experiencing, but to yield yourself totally to the Lord Jesus Christ and believe what God says in his Word. Do not attempt to crucify yourself; there are very few cases on record where a person has committed suicide by crucifixion! They usually select some other manner. It is equally impossible for you to carry out this crucifixion; God does not intend you to live by self-effort nor to grow spiritually by your own efforts. This is stated in Galatians 3:3, "Are ye so foolish, having begun in the Spirit, are ye now made perfect by the flesh?" Believe that God will honor his Word: "And ye shall know the truth and the truth shall make you free" (John 8:32). "Draw nigh to God and he will draw nigh to you" (James 4:8).

Each child of his is special in his sight, and he longs not to *help* them but to deliver them! A prisoner in a cell doesn't want help in the cell, he wants deliverance from it! David states in Psalm 142:7, "Bring my soul out of prison, that I may praise thy name..."

If you have surrendered *everything* and *everyone* in total submission to the perfect will of God, you can claim the promise of Psalm 50:14, 15: "Offer unto God thanksgiving; and pay thy vows unto the most high: And call upon me in the day of trouble; *I will deliver thee,* and thou shalt glorify *me.*" His purpose in delivering you from self, and the misery which emanates from it, is not *just* that you might be joyful and comfortable but that he might be glorified.

You must also become a student of his Word if you are to know "What is the riches of this mystery ... which is *Christ in you,* the hope of glory" (Colossians 1:27). Another way that Paul expressed this is in Galatians 2:20: "I am crucified with Christ; nevertheless I live; yet not I, but Christ liveth in me: and the life which I now live in the flesh I live by the faith of the Son of God, who loved me, and gave himself for me."

May God himself challenge you to appropriate your resources in the Lord Jesus Christ!

"And the peace of God, which passeth all understanding, shall keep your hearts and minds through Christ Jesus" (Philippians 4:7).

JOURNEY TO THE END OF SELF

When I came to Jesus
For the cleansing of my sin, (John 3:3)
My heart was set at peace
As the Saviour came within. (2 Cor. 5:17)

Looking to his promise
Of a life of victory, (2 Cor. 2:14)
My faith was sadly taxed,
As I struggled to be free. (Rom. 7:24, 25)

The burdens that I bore
Were heavier day by day;
It seemed God didn't care (Ps. 142:4)
As I labored in the way.

I searched for other means
For relief from trials sore;
No comfort could I find
And I yielded to him more. (Rom. 12:1)

My Lord had heard my cry (Ps. 142)
And began to guide my way; (Ps. 37:5)
Tho' comfort was not giv'n
He refused to let me stray.

My strength was well nigh gone,
And continued to decrease;
Until there was no more
And he gave to me his peace. (John 14:27)

My heart was filled with peace
That passeth understanding; (Phil. 4:6, 7)
I knelt in heartfelt awe
My soul was not demanding.

Tho' pain had been my lot, (Phil. 1:29, 30)
In his suff'ring I was blest; (Phil. 3:10)
Crucified with Christ, (Gal. 2:20)
I have found in him my rest. (Matt. 11:28, 29)

C. R. SOLOMON

Suggestions for Additional Study

Captain Reginald Wallis, *The New Life*, Loizeaux Brothers

Miles J. Stanford, *Principles of Spiritual Growth*, Back to the Bible Broadcast

Norman B. Harrison, *New Testament Living*, His International Service, *His Side Versus Our Side*, His International Service

F. B. Meyer, *The Christ Life for Your Life*, Moody Press

Mr. and Mrs. Howard Taylor, *Hudson Taylor's Spiritual Secret*, Moody Press

V. Raymond Edman, *They Found the Secret*, Zondervan

Watchman Nee, *The Normal Christian Life*, Christian Literature Crusade, *Sit, Walk, Stand*, Christian Literature Crusade

Ruth Paxson, *Life on the Highest Plane*, Moody Press, *Rivers of Living Water*, Moody Press

William R. Newell, *Romans Verse by Verse*, Moody Press

James McConkey, *The Three-Fold Secret of the Holy Spirit*, Back to the Bible Broadcast

T. Austin Sparks, *What is Man?*, Premium Literature Co., Box 18505, Indianapolis, Indiana

Andrew Murray, *Abide in Christ*, Keats, *Absolute Surrender*, Christian Literature Crusade, *The New Life*, Bethany Fellowship, *The True Vine*, Moody Press

C. S. Lovett, *Dealing with the Devil*, Personal Christianity, Baldwin Park, California

Theodore H. Epp, *The Other Comforter*, Back to the Bible Broadcast

F. J. Huegel, *Bone of His Bone*, Zondervan

Victor Matthews, *Growth in Grace*, Zondervan

EPILOGUE

God has proven the validity of this approach to Christian counseling in setting many persons free from most forms of "mental illness" since the incorporation of Grace Fellowship International in May 1969. It is clear now that he would establish Spirituotherapy as a new discipline to replace psychotherapy and psychiatry for anyone who wants, or is willing to consider, God's answer to his problem.

Implicit in such a task is the development of training programs at many levels of proficiency for both the layman and the professional counselor. Certification will be provided which is appropriate for the level and extent of training completed. A correspondence course is being developed so that persons may do the academic portion of their training at their place of residence. The length of time in residence at GFI will depend on the type of certification desired. Short term institutes, conferences, workshops, and rotations are presently available. Those desiring credit toward degree programs will be accepted on a selective basis. Inquiries regarding training may be directed to GFI at 200 South Sheridan, Denver, Colorado 80226.

Since GFI is dedicated to the proposition that spiritual counseling is the responsibility of the local church, it is vital that pastors and ministerial students be given the training to prepare them for this task. To accomplish this, GFI staff is available to hold one- to three-day training sessions wherever there is ample interest and a key person to do the organizational work.

The implementation of such a task is solely dependent upon the living God who is fully able to perform that which he has promised (Romans 4:23, 24).

As in any task it can only be accomplished as God supplies the necessary personnel and funds. It is his work, and it is not intended that funds nor personnel will be solicited. All gifts are tax-deductible.

In addition to the training of counselors, a national "hot line" for helping those in need and for making referrals to those of like persuasion is envisioned as God provides for expansion of the ministry.

We earnestly covet your prayer that God will guide his work and supply the necessary men and women of every race and the funds and facilities with which to train them.

"Now unto him that is able to do exceeding abundantly above all that we ask or think, according to the power that worketh in us ..." (Ephesians 3:20).